BLACK LEGACY PRESS™

WWW.BLACKLEGACYPRESS.ORG

SLAVE NARRATIVES

VOLUME V
INDIANA NARRATIVES

By
United States.
Work Projects Administration

ISBN: 978-1-63652-219-7

SLAVE NARRATIVES

A Folk History of Slavery in the United States.
From Interviews with Former Slaves

UNITED STATES.
WORK PROJECTS ADMINISTRATION

TYPEWRITTEN RECORDS PREPARED BY
THE FEDERAL WRITERS' PROJECT
1936-1938
ASSEMBLED BY
THE LIBRARY OF CONGRESS PROJECT
WORK PROJECTS ADMINISTRATION
FOR THE DISTRICT OF COLUMBIA
SPONSORED BY THE LIBRARY OF
CONGRESS

WASHINGTON 1941

VOLUME V
INDIANA NARRATIVES

Prepared by
The Federal Writers' Project of
The Works Progress Administration
For the State of Georgia

CONTENTS

Ex-Slave Stories
District No. 5
Vanderburgh County
Lauana Creel

AN UNHAPPY EXPERIENCE
[GEORGE W. ARNOLD]

GEORGE W. ARNOLD

This is written from an interview with each of the following: George W. Arnold, Professor W.S. Best of the Lincoln High School and Samuel Bell, all of Evansville, Indiana.

George W. Arnold was born April 7, 1861, in Bedford County, Tennessee. He was the property of Oliver P. Arnold, who owned a large farm or plantation in Bedford county. His mother was a native of Rome, Georgia, where she remained until twelve years of age, when she was sold at auction.

Oliver Arnold bought her, and he also purchased her three brothers and one uncle. The four negroes were taken along with other slaves from Georgia to Tennessee where they were put to work on the Arnold plantation.

On this plantation George W. Arnold was born and the child was allowed to live in a cabin with his relatives and declares that he never heard one of them speak an unkind word about Master Oliver Arnold or any member of his family. "Happiness and contentment and a reasonable amount of food and clothes seemed to be all we needed," said the now white-haired man.

Only a limited memory of Civil War days is retained by the old man but the few events recalled are vividly described by him. "Mother, my young brother, my sister and I were walking along one day. I don't remember where we had started but we passed under the fort at Wartrace. A battle was in progress and a large cannon was fired above us and we watched the huge ball sail through the air and saw the smoke of the cannon pass over our heads. We poor children were almost scared to death but our mother held us close to her and tried to comfort us. The next morning, after, we were safely at home ... we were proud we had seen that much of the great battle and our mother told us the war was to give us freedom."

"Did your family rejoice when they were set free?" was the natural question to ask Uncle George.

"I cannot say that they were happy, as it broke up a lot of real friendships and scattered many families. Mother had a great many pretty quilts and a lot of bedding. After the negroes were set free, Mars. Arnold told us we could all go and make ourselves homes, so we started out, each of the grown persons loaded with great bundles of bedding, clothing and personal belongings. We walked all the way to Wartrace to try to find a home and some way to make a living."

George W. Arnold remembers seeing many soldiers going to the pike road on their way to Murfreesboro. "Long lines of tired men passed through Guy's Gap on their way to Murfreesboro," said he. "Older people said that they were sent out to pick up the dead from the battle fields after the bloody battle of Stone's river that had lately been fought at Murfreesboro. They took their comrades to bury them at the Union Cemetery near the town of Murfreesboro."

"Wartrace was a very nice place to make our home. It was located on the Nashville and Chattanooga and St. Louis railroad, just fifty-one miles from Nashville not many miles from our old home. Mother found work and we got along very well but as soon as we children were old enough to work, she went back to her old home in Georgia where a few years later she died. I believe she lived to be seventy-five or seventy six years of age, but I never saw her after she went back to Georgia."

"My first work was done on a farm (there are many fine farms in Tennessee) and although farm labor was not very profitable we were always fed wherever we worked and got some wages. Then I got a job on the railroad. Our car was side tracked at a place called Silver Springs," said Uncle George, "and right at that place came trouble that took the happiness out of my life forever." Here the story teller paused to collect his thoughts and conquer the nervous twitching of his lips. "It was like this: Three of us boys worked together. We were like three brothers, always sharing our fortunes with each other. We should never have done it, but we had made a habit of sending to Nashville after each payday and having a keg of Holland rum sent in by freight. This liquor was handed out among our friends and sometimes we drank too much and were unfit for work for a day or two. Our boss was a big strong Irishman, red haired and friendly. He always got drunk with us and all would become sober enough to soon return to our tasks."

"The time I'm telling you about, we had all been invited to a candy pulling in town and could hardly wait till time to go, as all the young people of the valley would be there to pull candy, talk, play games and eat the goodies served to us. The accursed keg of Holland rum had been brought in that morning and my chum John Sims had been drinking too much. About that time our Boss came up and said, 'John, it is time for you to get the supper ready!' John was our cook and our meals were served on the caboose where we lived wherever we were side tracked."

"All the time Johny was preparing the food he was drinking the rum. When we went in he had many drinks inside of him and a quart bottle filled to take to the candy pull. 'Hurry up boys and let's finish up and go' he said impatiently. 'Don't take him' said the other boy, 'Dont you see he is drunk?' So I put my arms about his shoulders and tried to tell him he had better sleep a while before we started. The poor boy was a breed. His mother was almost white and his father was a thoroughbred Indian and the son had a most aggravating temper. He made me no answer but running his hand into his pocket, he drew out his knife and with one thrust, cut a deep gash in my neck. A terrible fight followed. I remember being knocked over and my head stricking something. I reached out my hand and discovered it was the ax. With this awful weapon I struck my friend, my more than brother. The thud of the ax brought me to my senses as our blood mingled. We were both almost mortally wounded. The boss came in and tried to do something for our relief but John said, 'Oh, George? what an awful thing we have done? We have never said a cross word to each other and now, look at us both.'"

"I watched poor John walk away, darkness was falling but early in the morning my boss and I followed a trail of blood down by the side of the tracks. From there he had turned into the woods. We could follow him no further. We went to all the nearby towns and villages but we found no person who had ever seen him. We supposed he had died in the woods and watched for the buzzards, thinking thay would lead us to his body but he was never seen again."

"For two years I never sat down to look inside a book nor to eat my food that John Sims was not beside me. He haunted my pillow and went beside me night and day. His blood was on my hands, his presence haunted me beyond endurance. What could I do? How could I escape this awful presence? An old friend told me to put water between myself and the place where the awful scene occurred. So, I quit working on the railroad and started working on the river. People believed at that time that the ghost of a person you had wronged would not cross water to haunt you."

Life on the river was diverting. Things were constantly happening and George Arnold put aside some of his unhappiness by engaging in river activities.

"My first job on the river was as a roust-about on the Bolliver H Cook a stern wheel packet which carried freight and passengers from Nashville, Tennessee to Evansville, Indiana. I worked a round trip on her and then went from Nashville to Cairo, Illinois on the B.S. Rhea. I soon decided to go to Cairo and take a place on the Eldarado, a St. Louis and Cincinnati packet which crused from Cairo to Cincinnati. On that boat I worked as a roust-about for nearly three years."

"What did the roust-about have to do?" asked a neigh-bor lad who had come into the room. "The roust-about is no better than the mate that rules him. If the mate is kindly disposed the roust-about has an easy enough life. The negroes had only a few years of freedom and resent-ed cruelty. If the mate became too mean, a regular fight would follow and perhaps several roust-abouts would be hurt before it was finished."

Uncle George said that food was always plentiful on the boats. Passengers and freight were crowded together on the decks. At night there would be singing and dancing and fiddle music. "We roust-abouts would get together and shoot craps, dance or play cards until the call came to shuffle freight, then we would all get busy and the mate's voice giving orders could be heard for a long distance."

"In spite of these few pleasures, the life of a roust-about is the life of a dog. I do not recall any unkindnesses of slavery days. I was too young to realize what it was all about, but it could never have equalled the cruelty shown the laborer on the river boats by cruel mates and over-seers."

Another superstition advanced itself in the story of a boat, told by Uncle George Arnold. The story follows: "When I was a roust-about on the Gold Dust we were sailing out from New Orleans and as soon as we got well out on the broad stream the rats commenced jumping over board. 'See these rats' said an old river man, 'This boat will never make a return trip!'"

"At every port some of our crew left the boat but the mate and the captain said they were all fools and begged us to stay. So a few of us stayed to do the necessary work but the rats kept leaving as fast as they could."

"When the boat was nearing Hickman, Kentucky, we smelled fire, and by the time we were in the harbor passengers were being held to keep them from jumping overboard. Then the Captain told us boys to jump into the water and save ourselves. Two of us launched a bale of cotton overboard and jumped onto it. As we paddled away we had to often go under to put out the fires as our clothing would blaze up under the flying brands that fell upon our bodies."

"The burning boat was docked at Hickman. The passengers were put ashore but none of the freight was saved, and from a nearby willow thicket my matey and I watched the Gold Dust burn to the water's edge."

"Always heed the warnings of nature," said Uncle George, "If you see rats leaving a ship or a house prepare for a fire."

George W. Arnold said that Evansville was quite a nice place and a steamboat port even in the early days of his boating experiences and he decided to make his home here. He located in the town in 1880. "The Court House was located at Third and Main streets. Street cars were mule drawn and people thought it great fun to ride them." He recalls the first shovel full of dirt being lifted when the new Courthouse was being erected, and when it was finished two white men finishing the slate roof, fell to their death in the Court House yard.

George W. Arnold procured a job as porter in a wholesale feed store on May 10, 1880. John Hubbard and Company did business at the place, at this place he worked thirty seven years. F.W. Griese, former mayor of Evansville has often befriended the negro man and is ready to speak a kindly word in his praise. But the face of John Sims still presents itself when George Arnold is alone. "Never do anything to hurt any other person," says he, "The hurt always comes back to you."

George Arnold was married to an Evansville Woman, but two years ago he became a widower when death claimed his mate. He is now lonely, but were it not for a keg of Holland gin his old age would be spent in peace and happiness. "Beware of strong drink," said Uncle George, "It causes trouble."

Emery Turner
District #5
Lawrence County
Bedford, Indiana

REMINISCENCES OF TWO EX-SLAVES
THOMAS ASH, Mitchell, Ind.
MRS. MARY CRANE, Warren St., Mitchell, Ind.

THOMAS ASH

I have no way of knowing exactly how old I am, as the old Bible containing a record of my birth was destroyed by fire, many years ago, but I believe I am about eighty-one years old. If so, I must have been born sometime during the year, 1856, four years before the outbreak of the War Between The States. My mother was a slave on the plantation, or farm of Charles Ash, in Anderson county, Kentucky, and it was there that I grew up.

I remember playing with Ol' Massa's (as he was called) boys, Charley, Jim and Bill. I also have an unpleasant memory of having seen other slaves on the place, tied up to the whipping post and flogged for disobeying some order although I have no recollection of ever having been whipped myself as I was only a boy. I can also remember how the grown-up negroes on the place left to join the Union Army as soon as they learned of Lincoln's proclamation making them free men.

Ed. Note—Mr. Ash was sick when interviewed and was not able to do much talking. He had no picture of himself but agreed to pose for one later on. [TR: no photograph found.]

MRS. MARY CRANE

I was born on the farm of Wattie Williams, in 1855 and am eighty-two years old. I came to Mitchell, Indiana, about fifty years ago with my husband, who is now dead and four children and have lived here ever since. I was only a girl, about five or six years old when the Civil War broke out but I can remember very well, happenings of that time.

My mother was owned by Wattie Williams, who had a large farm, located in Larue county, Kentucky. My father was a slave on the farm of a Mr. Duret, nearby.

In those days, slave owners, whenever one of their

daughters would get married, would give her and her husband a slave as a wedding present, usually allowing the girl to pick the one she wished to accompany her to her new home. When Mr. Duret's eldest daughter married Zeke Samples, she choose my father to accompany them to their home.

Zeke Samples proved to be a man who loved his toddies far better than his bride and before long he was "broke". Everything he had or owned, including my father, was to be sold at auction to pay off his debts.

In those days, there were men who made a business of buying up negroes at auction sales and shipping them down to New Orleans to be sold to owners of cotton and sugar cane plantations, just as men today, buy and ship cattle. These men were called "Nigger-traders" and they would ship whole boat loads at a time, buying them up, two or three here, two or three there, and holding them in a jail until they had a boat load. This practice gave rise to the expression, "sold down the river."

My father was to be sold at auction, along with all of the rest of Zeke Samples' property. Bob Cowherd, a neighbor of Matt Duret's owned my grandfather, and the old man, my grandfather, begged Col. Bob to buy my father from Zeke Samples to keep him from being "sold down the river." Col. Bob offered what he thought was a fair price for my father and a "nigger-trader" raised his bid "25 [TR: $25?]. Col. said he couldn't afford to pay that much and father was about to be sold to the "nigger-trader" when his father told Col. Bob that he had $25 saved up and that if he would buy my father from Samples and keep the "nigger-trader" from getting him he would give him the money. Col. Bob Cowherd took my grandfather's $25 and offered to meet the traders offer and so my father was sold to him.

The negroes in and around where I was raised were not treated badly, as a rule, by their masters. There was one slave owner, a Mr. Heady, who lived nearby, who treated his slave worse than any of the other owners but I never heard of anything so awfully bad, happening to his "niggers". He had one boy who used to come over to our place and I can remember hearing Massa Williams call to my grandmother, to cook "Christine, give Heady's Doc something to eat. He looks hungry." Massa Williams always said "Heady's Doc" when speaking of him or any other slave, saying to call him, for instance, Doc Heady would sound as if he were Mr. Heady's own son and he said that wouldn't sound right.

When President Lincoln issued his proclamation, freeing the negroes, I remember that my father and most all of the other younger slave men left the farms to join the Union army. We had hard times then for awhile and had lots of work to do. I don't remember just when I first regarded myself as "free" as many of the negroes didn't understand just what it was all about.

Ed. Note: Mrs. Crane will also pose for a picture.

Submitted by:
William Webb Tuttle
District No. 2
Muncie, Indiana

SLAVES IN DELAWARE COUNTY
ROSA BARBER
812 South Jefferson
Muncie, Indiana

ROSA BARBER

Rosa Barber was born in slavery on the Fox Ellison plantation at North Carden[TR:?], in North Carolina, in the year 1861. She was four [HW: ?] years old when freed, but had not reached the age to be of value as a slave. Her memory is confined to that short childhood there and her experiences of those days and immediately after the Civil War must be taken from stories related to her by her parents in after years, and these are dimly retained.

Her maiden name was Rosa Fox Ellison, taken as was the custom, from the slave-holder who held her as a chattel. Her parents took her away from the plantation when they were freed and lived in different localities, supported by the father who was now paid American wages. Her parents died while she was quite young and she married Fox Ellison, an ex-slave of the Fox Ellison plantation. His name was taken from the same master as was hers. She and her husband lived together forty-three years, until his death. Nine children were born to them of which only one survives. After this ex-slave husband died Rosa Ellison married a second time, but this second husband died some years ago and she now remains a widow at the age of seventy-six years. She recalls that the master of the Fox Ellison plantation was spoken of as practicing no extreme discipline on his slaves. Slaves, as a prevailing business policy of the holder, were not allowed to look into a book, or any printed matter, and Rosa had no pictures or printed charts given her. She had to play with her rag dolls, or a ball of yarn, if there happened to be enough of old string to make one. Any toy or plaything was allowed that did not point toward book-knowledge. Nursery rhymes and folk-lore stories were censured severely and had to be confined to events that conveyed no uplift, culture or propaganda, or that conveyed no knowledge, directly or indirectly. Especially did they bar the mental polishing of the three R's. They could not prevent the vocalizing of music in the fields and the slaves found consolation there in pouring out their souls in unison with the songs of the birds.

Federal Writers' Project
of the W.P.A.
District #6
Marion County
Anna Pritchett
1200 Kentucky Avenue, Indianapolis, Indiana

FOLKLORE
MRS. MITTIE BLAKELEY—EX-SLAVE
2055 Columbia Avenue, Indianapolis, Indiana

MRS. MITTIE BLAKELEY

Mrs. Blakeley was born, in Oxford, Missouri, in 1858.

Her mother died when Mittie was a baby, and she was taken into the "big house" and brought up with the white children. She was always treated very kindly.

Her duties were the light chores, which had to be well done, or she was chided, the same as the white children would have been.

Every evening the children had to collect the eggs. The child, who brought in the most eggs, would get a ginger cake. Mittie most always got the cake.

Her older brothers and sisters were treated very rough, whipped often and hard. She said she hated to think, much less talk about their awful treatment.

When she was old enough, she would have to spin the

wool for her mistress, who wove the cloth to make the family clothes.

She also learned to knit, and after supper would knit until bedtime.

She remembers once an old woman slave had displeased her master about something. He had a pit dug, and boards placed over the hole. The woman was made to lie on the boards, face down, and she was beaten until the blood gushed from her body; she was left there and bled to death.

She also remembers how the slaves would go to some cabin at night for their dances; if one went without a pass, which often they did, they would be beaten severely.

The slaves could hear the overseers, riding toward the cabin. Those, who had come without a pass, would take the boards up from the floor, get under the cabin floor, and stay there until the overseers had gone.

Interviewer's Comment

Mrs. Blakeley is very serious and said she felt so sorry for those, who were treated so such worse than any human would treat a beast.

She lives in a very comfortable clean house, and said she was doing "very well."

Submitted January 24, 1938
Indianapolis, Indiana

Submitted by:
Robert C. Irvin
District No. 2
Noblesville, Ind.

SLAVES IN MADISON COUNTY
CARL BOONE
Anderson, Indiana

CARL BOONE

This is a story of slavery, told by Carl Boone about his father, his mother and himself. Carl is the last of eighteen children born to Mrs. Stephen Boone, in Marion County, Kentucky, Sept. 15, 1850. He now resides with his children at 801 West 13th Street, Anderson, Madison County, Indiana. At the ripe old age of eighty-seven, he still has a keen memory and is able to do a hard day's work.

Carl Boone was born a free man, fifteen years before the close of the Civil War, his father having gained his freedom from slavery in 1829. He is a religious man, having missed church service only twice in twenty years. He was treated well during the time of slavery in the southland, but remembers well, the wrongs done to slaves on neighboring plantations, and in this story he relates some of the horrors which happened at that time.

Like his father, he is also the father of eighteen children, sixteen of whom are still living. He is grandfather of thirty-seven and great grandfather of one child. His father was born in the slave state of Maryland, in 1800, and died in 1897. His mother was born in Marion County, Kentucky, in 1802, and died in 1917, at the age of one hundred and fifteen years.

This story, word by word, is related by Carl Boone as follows: "My name is Carl Boone, son of Stephen and Rachel Boone, born in Marion County, Kentucky, in 1850. I am father of eighteen children sixteen are still living and I am grandfather of thirty-seven and great grandfather of one child. I came with my wife, now deceased, to Indiana, in 1891, and now reside at 801 West 13th street in Anderson, Indiana. I was born a free man, fifteen years before the close of the Civil War. All the colored folk on plantations and farms around our plantation were slaves and most of them were terribly mistreated by their masters.

After coming to Indiana, I farmed for a few years, then moved to Anderson. I became connected with the Colored Catholic Church and have tried to live a Christian life. I have only missed church service twice in twenty years. I lost my dear wife thirteen years ago and I now live with my son.

My father, Stephen Boone, was born in Maryland, in 1800. He was bought by a nigger buyer while a boy and was sold to Miley Boone in Marion County, Kentucky. Father was what they used to call "a picked slave," was a good worker and was never mistreated by his master. He married my mother in 1825, and they had eighteen children. Master Miley Boone gave father and mother their freedom in 1829, and gave them forty acres of land to tend as their own. He paid father for all the work he did for him after that, and was always very kind to them.

My mother was born in slavery, in Marion County, Kentucky, in 1802. She was treated very mean until she married my father in 1825. With him she gained her freedom in 1829. I was the last born of her eighteen children. She was a good woman and joined church after coming to Indiana and died in 1917, living to be one hundred and fifteen years old.

I have heard my mother tell of a girl slave who worked in the kitchen of my mother's master. The girl was told to cook twelve eggs for breakfast. When the eggs were served, it was discovered there were eleven eggs on the table and after being questioned, she admitted that she had eaten one. For this, she was beaten mercilessly, which was a common sight on that plantation.

The most terrible treatment of any slave, is told by my father in a story of a slave on a neighboring plantation, owned by Daniel Thompson. "After committing a small wrong, Master Thompson became angry, tied his slave to a whipping post and beat him terribly. Mrs. Thompson begged him to quit whipping, saying, 'you might kill him,' and the master replied that he aimed to kill him. He then tied the slave behind a horse and dragged him over a fifty acre field until the slave was dead. As a punishment for this terrible deed, master Thompson was compelled to witness the execution of his own son, one year later. The story is as follows:

A neighbor to Mr. Thompson, a slave owner by name of Kay Van Cleve, had been having some trouble with one of his young male slaves, and had promised the slave a whipping. The slave was a powerful man and Mr. Van Cleve was afraid to undertake the job of whipping him alone. He called for help from his neighbors, Daniel Thompson and his son Donald. The slave, while the Thompsons were coming, concealed himself in a horse-stall in the barn and hid a large knife in the manger.

After the arrival of the Thompsons, they and Mr. Van Cleve entered the stall in the barn. Together, the three white men made a grab for the slave, when the slave suddenly made a lunge at the elder Mr. Thompson with the knife, but missed him and stabbed Donald Thompson.

The slave was overpowered and tied, but too late, young Donald was dead.

The slave was tried for murder and sentenced to be hanged. At the time of the hanging, the first and second ropes used broke when the trap was sprung. For a while the executioner considered freeing the slave because of his second failure to hang him, but the law said, "He shall hang by the neck until dead," and the third attempt was successful."

Federal Writers' Project
of the W.P.A.
District #6
Marion County
Anna Pritchett
1200 Kentucky Avenue, Indianapolis, Indiana

FOLKLORE
MRS. JULIA BOWMAN—EX-SLAVE
1210 North West Street, Indianapolis, Indiana

MRS. JULIA BOWMAN

Mrs. Bowman was born in Woodford County, Kentucky in 1859.

Her master, Joel W. Twyman was kind and generous to all of his slaves, and he had many of them.

The Twyman slaves were always spoken of, as the Twyman "Kinfolks."

All slaves worked hard on the large farm, as every kind of vegetation was raised. They were given some of everything that grew on the farm, therefore there was no stealing to get food.

The master had his own slaves, and the mistress had her own slaves, and all were treated very kindly.

Mrs. Bowman was taken into the Twyman "big house," at the age of six, to help the mistress in any way she could. She stayed in the house until slavery was abolished.

After freedom, the old master was taken very sick and some of the former slaves were sent for, as he wanted some of his "Kinfolks" around him when he died.

Interviewer's Comment

Mrs. Bowman was given the Twyman family bible where her birth is recorded with the rest of the Twyman family. She shows it with pride.

Mrs. Bowman said she never knew want in slave times, as she has known it in these times of depression.

Submitted January 10, 1938
Indianapolis, Indiana

Wm. R. Mays
Dist 4
Johnson Co.

ANGIE BOYCE
BORN IN SLAVERY, Mar. 14, 1861 on the
Breeding Plantation, Adair Co. Ky.

ANGIE BOYCE

M rs. Angie Boyce here makes mention of facts as outlined to her by her mother, Mrs. Margaret King, deceased.

Mrs. Angie Boyce was born in slavery, Mar. 14, 1861, on the Breeding Plantation, Adair County, Kentucky. Her parents were Henry and Margaret King who belonged to James Breeding, a Methodist minister who was kind to all his slaves and no remembrance of his having ever struck one of them.

It is said that the slaves were in constant dread of the Rebel soldiers and when they would hear of their coming they would hide the baby "Angie" and cover her over with leaves.

The mother of Angie was married twice; the name of her first husband was Stines and that of her second husband was Henry King. It was Henry King who bought his and his wife's freedom. He sent his wife and baby Angie to Indiana, but upon their arrival they were arrested and returned to Kentucky. They were placed in the Louisville jail and lodged in the same cell with large Brutal and drunken Irish woman. The jail was so infested with bugs and fleas that the baby Angie cryed all night. The white woman crazed with drink became enraged at the cries of the child and threatened to "bash its brains out against the wall if it did not stop crying". The mother, Mrs. King was forced to stay awake all night to keep the white woman from carrying out her threat.

The next morning the Negro mother was tried in court and when she produced her free papers she was asked why she did not show these papers to the arresting officers. She replied that she was afraid that they would steal them from her. She was exonerated from all charges and sent back to Indiana with her baby.

Mrs. Angie Boyce now resides at 498 W. Madison St., Franklin, Ind.

Special Assignment
Walter R. Harris
District #3
Clay County

LIFE STORY OF EX-SLAVE
MRS. EDNA BOYSAW

MRS. EDNA BOYSAW

Mrs. Boysaw has been a citizen of this community about sixty-five years. She resides on a small
farm, two miles east of Brazil on what is known
as the Pinkley Street Road. This has been her home for
the past forty years. Her youngest son and the son of one
of her daughters lives with her. She is still very active,
doing her housework and other chores about the farm.
She is very intelligent and according to statements made
by other citizens has always been a respected citizen
in the community, as also has her entire family. She is
the mother of twelve children. Mrs. Boysaw has always
been an active church worker, spending much time in
missionary work for the colored people. Her work was
so outstanding that she has been often called upon to
speak, not only in the colored churches, but also in white
churches, where she was always well received. Many of
the most prominent people of the community number
Mrs. Boysaw as one of their friends and her home is visited almost daily by citizens in all walks of life. Her many
acts of kindness towards her neighbors and friends have
endeared her to the people of Brazil, and because of her

long residence in the community, she is looked upon as one of the pioneers.

Mrs. Boysaw's husband has been dead for thirty-five years. Her children are located in various cities throughout the country. She has a daughter who is a talented singer, and has appeared on programs with her daughter in many churches. She is not certain about her age, but according to her memory of events, she is about eighty-seven.

Her story as told to the writer follows:

"When the Civil War ended, I was living near Richmond, Virginia. I am not sure just how old I was, but I was a big, flat-footed woman, and had worked as a slave on a plantation. My master was a good one, but many of them were not. In a way, we were happy and contented, working from sun up to sun down. But when Lincoln freed us, we rejoiced, yet we knew we had to seek employment now and make our own way. Wages were low. You worked from morning until night for a dollar, but we did not complain. About 1870 a Mr. Masten, who was a coal operator, came to Richmond seeking laborers for his mines in Clay County. He told us that men could make four to five dollars a day working in the mines, going to work at seven and quitting at 3:30 each day. That sounded like a Paradise to our men folks. Big money and you could get rich in little time. But he did not tell all, because he wanted the men folk to come with him to Indiana. Three or four hundred came with Mr. Masten. They were brought in box cars. Mr. Masten paid their transportation, but was to keep it out of their wages. My husband was in that bunch, and the women folk stayed behind until their men could earn enough for their transportation to Indiana."

"When they arrived about four miles east of Brazil, or what was known as Harmony, the train was stopped and a crowd of white miners ordered them not to come any nearer Brazil. Then the trouble began. Our men did not know of the labor trouble, as they were not told of that part. Here they were fifteen hundred miles from home, no money. It was terrible. Many walked back to Virginia. Some went on foot to Illinois. Mr. Masten took some of them South of Brazil about three miles, where he had a number of company houses, and they tried to work in his mine there. But many were shot at from the bushes and killed. Guards were placed about the mine by the owner, but still there was trouble all the time. The men did not make what Mr. Masten told them they could make, yet they had to stay for they had no place to go. After about six months, my husband who had been working in that mine, fell into the shaft and was injured. He was unable to work for over a year. I came with my two children to take care of him. We had only a little furniture, slept in what was called box beds. I walked to Brazil each morning and worked at whatever I could get to do. Often did three washings a day and then walked home each evening, a distance of two miles, and got a dollar a day.

"Many of the white folks I worked for were well to do and often I would ask the Mistress for small amounts of food which they would throw out if left over from a meal. They did not know what a hard time we were having, but they told me to take home any of such food that I cared to. I was sure glad to get it, for it helped to feed our family. Often the white folks would give me other articles which I appreciated. I managed in this way to get the children enough to eat and later when my husband was able to work, we got along very well, and were thankful. After the strike was settled, things were better. My husband was not afraid to go out after dark. But the coal operators did not treat the colored folks very good. We had to trade at the Company store and often pay a big price for it. But I worked hard and am still alive today, while all the others are gone, who lived around here about that time. There has sure been a change in the country. The country was almost a wilderness, and where my home is today, there were very few roads, just what we called a pig path through the woods. We used lots of corn meal, cooked beans and raised all the food we could during them days. But we had many white friends and sure was thankful for them. Here I am, and still thankful for the many friends I have."

Federal Writers' Project
of the W.P.A.
District #6
Marion County
Anna Pritchett
1200 Kentucky Avenue, Indianapolis, Indiana

FOLKLORE
MRS. CALLIE BRACEY—DAUGHTER [of Louise Terrell]
414 Blake Street

MRS. CALLIE BRACEY

Mrs. Callie Bracey's mother, Louise Terrell, was bought, when a child, by Andy Ramblet, a farmer, near Jackson, Miss. She had to work very hard in the fields from early morning until as late in the evening, as they could possibly see.

No matter how hard she had worked all day after coming in from the field, she would have to cook for the next day, packing the lunch buckets for the field hands. It made no difference how tired she was, when the horn was blown at 4 a.m., she had to go into the field for another day of hard work.

The women had to split rails all day long, just like the men. Once she got so cold, her feet seemed to be frozen; when they warmed a little, they had swollen so, she could not wear her shoes. She had to wrap her foot in burlap, so she would be able to go into the field the next day.

The Ramblets were known for their good butter. They always had more than they could use. The master wanted the slaves to have some, but the mistress wanted to sell it, she did not believe in giving good butter to slaves and always let it get strong before she would let them have any.

No slaves from neighboring farms were allowed on the Ramblet farm, they would get whipped off as Mr. Ramblet did not want anyone to put ideas in his slave's heads.

On special occasions, the older slaves were allowed to go to the church of their master, they had to sit in the back of the church, and take no part in the service.

Louise was given two dresses a year; her old dress from last year, she wore as an underskirt. She never had a hat, always wore a rag tied over her head.

Interviewer's Comment

Mrs. Bracey is a widow and has a grandchild living with her. She feels she is doing very well, her parents had so little, and she does own her own home.

Submitted December 10, 1937
Indianapolis, Indiana

Ex-Slave Stories
District #5
Vanderburgh County
Lauana Creel

A SLAVE, AMBASSADOR AND CITY DOCTOR
[DR. GEORGE WASHINGTON BUCKNER]

DR. GEORGE WASHINGTON BUCKNER

This paper was prepared after several interviews had been obtained with the subject of this sketch.

Dr. George Washingtin [TR: Washington] Buckner, tall, lean, whitehaired, genial and alert, answered the call of his door bell. Although anxious to oblige the writer and willing to grant an interview, the life of a city doctor is filled with anxious solicitation for others and he is always expecting a summons to the bedside of a patient or a professional interview has been slated.

Dr. Buckner is no exception and our interviews were often disturbed by the jingle of the door bell or a telephone call.

Dr. Buckner's conversation lead in ever widening circles, away from the topic under discussion when the events of his own life were discussed, but he is a fluent speaker and a student of psychology. Psychology as that philosophy relates to the mental and bodily tendencies of the African race has long since become one of the major subjects with which this unusual man struggles. "Why is the negro?" is one of his deepest concerns.

Dr. Buckner's first recollections center within a slave cabin in Kentucky. The cabin was the home of his step-father, his invalid mother and several children. The cabin was of the crudest construction, its only windows being merely holes in the cabin wall with crude bark shutters arranged to keep out snow and rain. The furnishings of this home consisted of a wood bedstead upon which a rough straw bed and patchwork quilts provided meager comforts for the invalid mother. A straw bed that could be pushed under the bed-stead through the day was pulled into the middle of the cabin at night and the wearied children were put to bed by the impatient step-father.

The parents were slaves and served a master not wealthy enough to provide adaquately for their comforts. The mother had become invalidate through the task of bearing children each year and being deprived of medical and surgical attention.

The master, Mr. Buckner, along with several of his relatives had purchased a large tract of land in Green County, Kentucky and by a custom or tradition as Dr. Buckner remembers; land owners that owned no slaves were considered "Po' White Trash" and were scarcely recognized as citizens within the state of Kentucky.

Another tradition prevailed, that slave children should be presented to the master's young sons and daughters and become their special property even in childhood. Adherring to that tradition the child, George Washington Buckner became the slave of young "Mars" Dickie Buckner, and although the two children were nearly the same age the little mulatto boy was obedient to the wishes of the little master. Indeed, the slave child cared for the Caucasian boy's clothing, polished his boots, put away his toys and was his playmate and companion as well as his slave.

Sickness and suffering and even death visits alike the just and the unjust, and the loving sympathetic slave boy witnessed the suffering and death of his little white friend. Then grief took possession of the little slave, he could not bear the sight of little Dick's toys nor books not [TR: nor?] clothing. He recalls one harrowing experience after the death of little Dick Buckner. George's grandmother was a housekeeper and kitchen maid for the white family. She was in the kitchen one late afternoon preparing the evening meal. The master had taken his family for a visit in the neighborhood and the mulatto child sat on the veranda and recalled pleasanter days. A sudden desire seized him to look into the bed room where little Mars Dickie had lain in the bed. The evening shadows had fallen, exaggerated by the influence of trees, and vines, and when he placed his pale face near the window pane he thought it was the face of little Dickie looking out at him. His nerves gave away and he ran around the house screaming to his grandmother that he had seen Dickie's ghost. The old colored woman was sympathetic, dried his tears, then with tears coursing down her own cheeks she went about her duties. George firmly believed he had seen a ghost and never really convinced himself against the idea until he had reached the years of manhood. He remembers how the story reached the ears of the other slaves and they were terrorized at the suggestion of a ghost being in the master's home. "That is the way superstitions always started" said the Doctor,

"Some nervous persons received a wrong impression and there were always others ready to embrace the error."

Dr. Buckner remembers that when a young daughter of his master married, his sister was given to her for a bridal gift and went away from her own mother to live in the young mistress' new home. "It always filled us with sorrow when we were separated either by circumstances of marriage or death. Although we were not properly housed, properly nourished nor properly clothed we loved each other and loved our cabin homes and were unhappy when compelled to part."

"There are many beautiful spots near the Green River and our home was situated near Greensburgh, the county seat of Dreen [TR: Green?] County." The area occupied by Mr. Buckner and his relatives is located near the river and the meanderings of the stream almost formed a peninsula covered with rich soil. Buckner's hill relieved the landscape and clear springs bubled through crevices affording much water for household use and near those springs white and negro children met to enjoy themselves.

"Forty years after I left Greensburg I went back to visit the springs and try to meet my old friends. The friends had passed away, only a few merchants and salespeople remembered my ancestors."

A story told by Dr. Buckner relates an evening at the beginning of the Civil War. "I had heard my parents talk of the war but it did not seem real to me until one night when mother came to the pallet where we slept and called to us to 'Get up and tell our uncles good-bye.' Then four startled little children arose. Mother was standing in the room with a candle or a sort of torch made from grease drippings and old pieces of cloth, (these rude candles were in common use and afforded but poor light) and there stood her four brothers, Jacob, John, Bill, and Isaac all with the light of adventure shining upon their mulatto countenances. They were starting away to fight for their liberties and we were greatly impressed."

Dr. Buckner stated that officials thought Jacob entirely too aged to enter the service as he had a few scattered white hairs but he remembers he was brawny and unafraid. Isaac was too young but the other two uncles were accepted. One never returned because he was killed in battle but one fought throughout the war and was never wounded. He remembers how the white men were indignant because the negroes were allowed to enlist and how Mars Stanton Buckner was forced to hide out in the woods for many months because he had met slave Frank Buckner and had tried to kill him. Frank returned to Greensburg, forgave his master and procurred a paper stating that he was at fault, after which Stanton returned to active service. "Yes, the road has been long. Memory brings back those days and the love of my mother is still real to me, God bless her!"

Relating to the value of an education Dr. Buckner hopes every Caucassian and Afro-American youth and maiden will strive to attain great heights. His first efforts to procure knowledge consisted of reciting A.B.S.s [TR: A.B.C.s?] from the McGuffy's [HW: ?] Blue backed speller with his unlettered sister for a teacher. In later years he attended a school conducted by the Freemen's Association. He bought a grammar from a white school boy and studied it at home. When sixteen years of age he was employed to teach negro children and grieves to recall how limited his ability was bound to have been. "When a father considers sending his son or daughter to school, today, he orders catalogues, consults his friends and considers the location and surroundings and the advice of those who have patronized the different schools. He finally decides upon the school that promises the boy or girl the most attractive and comfortable surroundings. When I taught the African children I boarded with an old man whose cabin was filled with his own family. I climbed a ladder leading from the cabin into a dark uncomfortable loft where a comfort and a straw bed were my only conveniences."

Leaving Greensburg the young mulatto made his way to Indianapolis where he became acquainted with the first educated Negro he had ever met. The Negro was Robert Bruce Bagby, then principal of the only school for Negroes in Indianapolis. "The same old building is standing there today that housed Bagby's institution then," he declares.

Dr. Buckner recalls that when he left Bagby's school he was so low financially he had to procure a position in a private residence as house boy. This position was followed by many jobs of serving tables at hotels and eating houses, of any and all kinds. While engaged in that work he met Colonel Albert Johnson and his lovely wife, both natives of Arkansas and he remembers their congratulations when they learned that he was striving for an education. They advised his entering an educational institution at Terre Haute. His desire had been to enter that institution of Normal Training but felt doubtful of succeeding in the advanced courses taught because his advantages had been so limited, but Mrs. Johnson told him that "God gives his talents to the different species and he would love and protect the negro boy."

After studying several years at the Terre Haute State Normal George W. Buckner felt assured that he was reasonably prepared to teach the negro youths and accepted the professorship of schools at Vincennes, Washington and other Indiana Villages. "I was interested in the young people and anxious for their advancement but the suffering endured by my invalid mother, who had passed into the great beyond, and the memory of little Master Dickie's lingering illness and untimely death would not desert my consciousness. I determined to take up the study of medical practice and surgery which I did."

Dr. Buckner graduated from the Indiana Electic Medical College in 1890. His services were needed at Indianapolis so he practiced medicine in that city for a year, then located at Evansville where he has enjoyed an ever increasing popularity on account of his sympathetic attitude among his people.

"When I came to Evansville," says Dr. Buckner, "there were seventy white physicians practicing in the area, they are now among the departed. Their task was streneous, roads were almost impossible to travel and those brave men soon sacrificed their lives for the good of suffering humanity." Dr. Buckner described several of the old doctors as "Striding [TR: illegible handwritten word above 'striding'] a horse and setting out through all kinds of weather."

Dr. Buckner is a veritable encyclopedia of negro lore. He stops at many points during an interview to relate stories he has gleaned here and there. He has forgotten where he first heard this one or that one but it helps to illustrate a point. One he heard near the end of the war follows, and although it has recently been retold it holds the interest of the listener. "Andrew Jackson owned an old negro slave, who stayed on at the old home when his beloved master went into politics, became an American soldier and statesman and finally the 7th president of the United States. The good slave still remained through the several years of the quiet uneventful last years of his master and witnessed his death, which occurred at his home near Nashville, Tennessee. After the master had been placed under the sod, Uncle Sammy was seen each day visiting Jackson's grave.

"Do you think President Jackson is in heaven?" an acquaintance asked Uncle Sammy.

"If-n he wanted to go dar, he dar now," said the old man. "If-n Mars Andy wanted to do any thing all Hell couldn't keep him from doin' it."

Dr. Buckner believes each Negro is confident that he will take himself with all his peculiarities to the land of promise. Each physical feature and habitual idiosyncrasy will abide in his redeemed personality. Old Joe will be there in person with the wrinkle crossing the bridge of his nose and little stephen will wear his wool pulled back from his eyes and each will recognize his fellow man. "What fools we all are," declared Dr. Buckner.

Asked his views concerning the different books embraced in the Holy Bible, Dr. Buckner, who is a student of the Bible said, "I believe almost every story in the Bible is an allegory, composed to illustrate some fundamental truth that could otherwise never have been clearly presented only through the medium of an allegory."

"The most treacherous impulse of the human nature and the one to be most dreaded is jealousy." With these words the aged Negro doctor launched into the expression of his political views. "I'm a Democrat." He then explained how he voted for the man but had confidence that his chosen party possesses ability in choosing proper candidates. He is an ardent follower of Franklin D. Roosevelt and speaks of Woodrow Wilson with bated breath.

Through the influence of John W. Boehne, Sr., and the friendly advice of other influential citizens of Evansville Dr. Buckner was appointed minister to Liberia, on Woodrow Wilson's cabinet, in the year 1913. Dr. Buckner appreciated the confidence of his friends in appointing him and cherishes the experineces gained while abroad. He noted the expressions of gratitude toward cabinet members by the citizens of that African coast. One Albino youth brought an offering of luscious mangoes and desired to see the minister from the United States of America. Some natives presented palm oils. "The natives have been made to understand that the United States has given aid to Liberia in a financial way and the customs-service of the republic is temporarily administered headed by an American." "A thoroughly civilized Negro state does not exist in Liberia nor do I believe in any part of West Africa. Superstition is the interpretation of their religion, their political views are a hodgepodge of unconnected ideas. Strength over rules knowledge and jealousy crowds out almost all hope of sympathetic achievement and adjustment." Dr. Buckner recounted incidents where jealousy was apparent in the behavior of men and women of higher civilizations than the African natives. While voyaging to Spain on board a Spanish vessel, he witnessed a very refined, polite Jewish woman being reduced to tears by the taunts of a Spanish officer, on account of her nationality. "Jealousy," he said, "protrudes itself into politics, religion and prevents educational achievement."

During a political campaign I was compelled to pay a robust Negro man to follow me about my professional visits and my social evenings with my friends and family, to prevent meeting physical violence to myself or family when political factions were virtually at war within the area of Evansville. The influence of political captains had brought about the dreadful condition and ignorant Negroes responded to their political graft, without realizing who had befriended them in need."

"The negro youths are especially subject to propoganda of the four-flusher for their home influence is, to say the least, negative. Their opportunities limited, their education neglected and they are easily aroused by the meddling influence of the vote-getter and the traitor. I would to God that their eyes might be opened to the light."

Dr. Buckner's influence is mostly exhibited in the sick room, where his presence is introduced in the effort to relieve pain.

The gradual rise from slavery to prominence, the many trials encountered along the road has ripened the always sympathetic nature of Dr. Buckner into a responsive suffer among a suffering people. He has hope that proper influences and sympathetic advice will mould the plastic character of the Afro-American youths of the

United States into proper citizens and that their immortal souls inherit the promised reward of the redeemed through grace.

"Receivers of emancipation from slavery and enjoyers of emancipation from sin through the sacrifice of Abraham Lincoln and Jesus Christ; Why should not the negroes be exalted and happy?" are the words of Dr. Buckner.

Note: G.W. Buckner was born December 1st, 1852. The negroes in Kentucky expressed it, "In fox huntin' time" one brother was born in "Simmon time", one in "Sweet tater time," and another in "Plantin' time."

—Negro lore.

United States. Work Projects Administration

Ex-Slave Stories
District #5
Vanderburgh County
Lauana Creel

THE LIFE STORY OF GEORGE TAYLOR BURNS
[HW: Personal Interview]

GEORGE TAYLOR BURNS

Ox-carts and flat boats, and pioneer surroundings; crowds of men and women crowding to the rails of river steamboats; gay ladies in holiday attire and gentleman in tall hats, low cut vests and silk mufflers; for the excursion boats carried the gentry of every area.

A little negro boy clung to the ragged skirts of a slave mother, both were engrossed in watching the great wheels that ploughed the Mississippi river into foaming billows. Many boats stopped at Gregery's Landing, Missouri to stow away wood, for many engines were fired with wood in the early days.

The Burns brothers operated a wood yard at the Landing and the work of cutting, hewing and piling wood for the commerce was performed by slaves of the Burns plantation.

George Taylor Burns was five years of age and helped his mother all day as she toiled in the wood yards. "The colder the weather, the more hard work we had to do," declares Uncle George.

George Taylor Burns, the child of Missouri slave parents, recalls the scenes enacted at the Burns' wood yards so long ago. He is a resident of Evansville, Indiana and his snow white hair and beard bear testimony that his days have been already long upon the earth.

Uncle George remembers the time when his infant hands reached in vain for his mother, the kind and gentle Lucy Burns: Remembers a long cold winter of snow and ice when boats were tied up to their moorings. Old master died that winter and many slaves were sold by the heirs, among them was Lucy Burns. Little George clung to his mother but strong hands tore away his clasp. Then he watched her cross a distant hill, chained to a long line of departing slaves. George never saw his parents again and although the memory of his mother is vivid he scarcely remembers his father's face. He said, "Father was black but my mother was a bright mulatto."

Nothing impressed the little boy with such unforgettable imagery as the cold which descended upon Greogery's Landing one winter. Motherless, hungry, desolate and unloved, he often cried himself to sleep at night while each day he was compelled to carry wood. One morning he failed to come when the horn was sounded to call the slaves to breakfast. "Old Missus went to the Negro quarters to see what was wrong" and "She was horrified when she found I was frozen to the bed."

She carried the small bundle of suffering humanity to the kitchen of her home and placed him near the big oven. When the warmth thawed the frozen child the toes fell from his feet. "Old Missus told me I would never be strong enough to do hard work, and she had the neighborhood shoemaker fashion shoes too short for any body's feet but mine," said Uncle George.

Uncle George doesn't remember why he left Missouri but the sister of Greene Taylor brought him to Troy, Indiana. Here she learned that she could not own a slave within the State of Indiana so she indentured the child to a flat boat captain to wash dishes and wait on the crew of workers.

George was so small of stature that the captain had a low table and stool made that he might work in comfort. George's mistress received $15,00 [TR: $15.00?] per month for the service of the boy for several years.

From working on the flat boats George became accustomed to the river and soon received employment as a cabin boy on a steam boat and from that time through out the most active days of his life George Taylor Burns was a steam-boat man. In fact he declares, "I know steam-boats from wood box to stern wheel."

"The life of a riverman is a good life and interesting things happen on the river," says Uncle George.

Uncle George has been imprisoned in the big jail at New Orleans. He has seen his fellow slaves beaten into insensibility while chained to the whipping post in Congo Square at New Orleans.

He was badly treated while a slave but he has witnessed even more cruel treatment administered to his fellow slaves.

Among other exciting occurrences remembered by the old negro man when he recalls early river adventures is one in which a flat boat sunk near New Orleans. After clinging for many hours to the drifting wreckage he was rescued, half dead from exhaustion.

In memory, George Taylor Burns stands in the slave mart at New Orleans and hears the Auctioneers' hammer, for he was sold like a beast of burden by Greene Taylor, brother of his mistress. Greene Taylor, however, had to refund the money and return the slave to his mistress when his crippled feet were discovered.

"Greene Taylor was like many other people I have known. He was always ready to make life unhappy for a negro."

Uncle George, although possessing an unusual amount of intelligence and ability to learn, has a very limited education. "The Negroes were not allowed an education," he relates. "It was dangerous for any person to be caught teaching a Negro and several Negroes were put to death because they could read."

Uncle George recalls a few superstitions entertained by the rivermen. "It was bad luck for a white cat to come aboard the boat." "Horse shoes were carried for good luck." "If rats left the boat the crew was uneasy, for fear of a wreck." Uncle George has very little faith in any superstition but remembers some of the crews had.

Among other boats on which this old river man was employed are "The Atlantic" on which he was cabin boy. The "Big Gray Eagle" on which he assisted in many ways. He worked where boats were being constructed while he lived at New Albany.

Many soldiers were returned to their homes by means

of flat boats and steam boats when the Civil War had ended and many recruits were sent by water during the war. Just after peace was declared George met Elizabeth Slye, a young slave girl who had just been set free. "Liza would come to see her mother who was working on a boat." "People used to come down to the landings to see boats come in," said Uncle George. George and Liza were free, they married and made New Albany their home, until 1881 when they came to Evansville.

Uncle George said the Eclipse was a beautiful boat, he remembers the lettering in gold and the bright lights and polished rails of the longest steam boat ever built in the West. Measuring 365 feet in length and Uncle George declares, "For speed she just up and hustled."

"Louisville was one of the busiest towns in the Ohio Valley," says Uncle George, but he remembers New Orleans as the market place where almost all the surplus products were marketed.

Uncle George has many friends along the water-front towns. He admires the Felker family of Tell City, Indiana. He is proud of his own race and rejoices in their opportunities. He remembers his fear of the Ku Klux, his horror of the patrol and other clans united to make life dangerous for newly emancipated Negroes.

George Taylor Burns draws no old age pension. He owns a building located at Canal and Evans Streets that houses a number of Negro families. He is glad to say his credit is good in every market in the city. Although lamed by rheumatic pains and hobbling on feet toeless from his young childhood he has led a useful life. "Don't forget I knew Pilot Tom Ballard, and Aaron Ballard on the Big

Eagle in 1858," warns Uncle George. "We Negroes carried passes so we could save our skins if we were caught off the boats but we had plenty of good food on the boats."

Uncle George said the roustabouts sang gay songs while loading boats with heavy freight and provisions but on account of his crippled feet he could not be a roustabout.

Federal Writers' Project
of the W.P.A.
District #6
Marion County
Anna Pritchett
1200 Kentucky Avenue

FOLKLORE
MRS. BELLE BUTLER—DAUGHTER [of Chaney Mayer]
829 North Capitol Avenue

MRS. BELLE BUTLER

Interviewer's Comment

Belle Butler, the daughter of Chaney Mayer, tells of the hardships her mother endured during her days of slavery.

Interview

Chaney was owned by Jesse Coffer, "a mean old devil." He would whip his slaves for the slightest misdemeanor, and many times for nothing at all—just enjoyed seeing them suffer. Many a time Jesse would whip a slave, throw him down, and gouge his eyes out. Such a cruel act!

Chaney's sister was also a slave on the Coffer plantation. One day their master decided to whip them both. After whipping them very hard, he started to throw them down, to go after their eyes. Chaney grabbed one of his hands, her sister grabbed his other hand, each girl bit a finger entirely off of each hand of their master. This, of course, hurt him so very bad he had to stop their punish-ment and never attempted to whip them again. He told them he would surely put them in his pocket (sell them) if they ever dared to try *anthing like that again in life.

Not so long after their fight, Chaney was given to a daughter of their master, and her sister was given to another daughter and taken to Passaic County, N.C.

On the next farm to the Coffer farm, the overseers would tie the slaves to the joists by their thumbs, whip them unmercifully, then salt their backs to make them very sore.

When a slave slowed down on his corn hoeing, no matter if he were sick, or just very tired, he would get many lashes and a salted back.

One woman left the plantation without a pass. The overseer caught her and whipped her to death.

No slave was ever allowed to look at a book, for fear he might learn to read. One day the old mistress caught a slave boy with a book, she cursed him and asked him what he meant, and what he thought he could do with a book. She said he looked like a black dog with a breast pin on, and forbade him to ever look into a book again.

All slaves on the Coffer plantation were treated in a most inhuman manner, scarcely having enough to eat, unless they would steal it, running the risk of being caught and receiving a severe beating for the theft.

Interviewer's Comment

Mrs. Butler lives with her daughters, has worked very hard in "her days."

She has had to give up almost everything in the last few years, because her eyesight has failed. However, she is very cheerful and enjoys telling the "tales" her mother would tell her.

Submitted December 28, 1937
Indianapolis, Indiana

Ex-Slave Stories
5th District
Vandenburgh County
Lauana Creel

SLAVE STORY
JOSEPH WILLIAM CARTER

JOSEPH WILLIAM CARTER

This information was gained through an interview with Joseph William Carter and several of his daughters. The data was cheerfully given to the writer. Joseph William Carter has lived a long and, he declares, a happy life, although he was born and reared in bondage. His pleasing personality has always made his lot an easy one and his yoke seemed easy to wear.

Joseph William Carter was born prior to the year 1836. His mother, Malvina Gardner was a slave in the home of Mr. Gardner until a man named D.B. Smith saw her and noticing the physical perfection of the child at once purchased her from her master.

Malvina was agrieved at being compelled to leave her old home, and her lovely young mistress. Puss Gardner was fond of the little mullato girl and had taught her to be a useful member of the Gardner family; however, she was sold to Mr. Smith and was compelled to accompany him to his home.

Both the Gardner and Smith families lived near Gallatin, Tennessee, in Sumner County. The Smith plantation was situated on the Cumberland River and commanded a beautiful view of river and valley acres but Malvina was very unhappy. She did not enjoy the Smith family and longed for her old friends back in the Gardner home.

One night the little girl gathered together her few personal belongings and started back to her old home.

Afraid to travel the highway the child followed a path she knew through the forest; but alas, she found the way long and beset with perils. A number of uncivil Indians were encamped on the side of the Cumberland mountains and a number of the young braves were out hunting that night. Their stealthy approach was heard by the little fugitive girl but too late for her to make an escape. An Indian called "Buck" captured her and by all the laws of the tribe was his own property. She lived for almost a year in the teepe with Buck and during that time learned much about Indian habits.

When Malvina was missed from her new home, Mr. Smith went to the Gardner plantation to report his loss, not finding her there a wide search was made for her but the Indians kept her thoroughly concealed. Miss Puss, however, kept up the search. She knew the Indians were encamped on the mountain and believed she would find the girl with them. The Indians finally broke camp and the members of the Gardner home watched them start on their journey and Miss Puss soon discovered Malvina among the other maidens in the procession.

The men of the Gardner plantation, white and black, overtook the Indians and demanded the girl be given up to them. The Indians reluctantly gave her to them. Miss Puss Gardner took her back and Mr. Gardner paid Mr.

Smith the original purchase price and Malvina was once more installed in her old home.

Malvina Gardner was not yet twelve years of age when she was captured by the Indians and was scarcely thirteen years of age when she became the mother of Joseph William, son of the uncivil Indian, "Buck". The child was born in the Gardner home and mother and child remained there. The mother was a good slave and loved the members of the Gardner family and her son and she were loved by them in return.

Puss Gardner married a Mr. Mooney and Mr. Gardner allowed her to take Joseph William to her home. The Mooney estate was situated up on the Carthridge road and some of Joseph William's most vivid memories of slavery and the curse of bondage embrace his life's span with the Mooneys.

One story that the aged man relates is of an encounter with an eagle and follows: "George Irish, a white boy near my own age, was the son of the miller. His father operated a sawmill on Bledsoe Creek near where it empties into the Coumberland river. George and I often went fishing together and had a good dog called Hector. Hector was as good a coon dog as there was to be found in that part of the country. That day we boys climbed up on the mill shed to watch the swans in Bledsoe Creek and we soon noticed a great big fish hawk catching the goslings. It made us mad and we decided to kill the hawk. I went back to the house and got an old flint lock rifle Mars. Mooney had let me carry when we went hunting. When I got back where George was, the big bird was still busy catching goslings. The first shot I fired broke its wing and I decided I would catch it and take it home with me.

The bird put up a terrible fight, cutting me with its bill and talons. Hector came running and tried to help me but the bird cut him until his howls brought help from the field. Mr. Jacob Greene was passing along and came to us. He tore me away from the bird but I could not walk and the blood was running from my body in dozens of places. Poor old Hector, was crippled and bleeding for the bird was a big eagle and would have killed both of us if help had not come." The old negro man still shows signs of his encounter with the eagle. He said it was captured and lived about four months in captivity but its wing never healed. The body of the eagle was stuffed with wheat bran, by Greene Harris, and placed in the court yard in Sumner County. "The Civil War changed things at the Mooney plantation," said the old man. "Before the War Mr. Mooney never had been cruel to me. I was Mistress Puss's property and she would never have allowed me to be abused, but some of the other slaves endured the most cruel treatment and were worked nearly to death."

Uncle Joe's memory of slavery embraces the whole story of bondage and the helpless position held by strong bodied men and women of a hardy race, overpowered by the narrow ideals of slave owners and cruel overseerers. "When I was a little bitsy child and still lived with Mr. Gardner," said the old man, "I saw many of the slaves beaten to death. Master Gardner didn't do any of the whippin' but every few months he sent to Mississippi for negro rulers to come to the plantation and whip all the negroes that had not obeyed the overseers. A big barrel lay near the barn and that was always the whippin place." Uncle Joe remembers two or three professional slave whippers and recalls the death of two of the Mississippi whippers. He relates the story as follows: "Mars

Gardner had one of the finest black smiths that I ever saw. His arms were strong, his muscles stood out on his breast and shoulders and his legs were never tired. He stood there and shoed horses and repaired tools day after day and there was no work ever made him tired."

The old negro man so vividly described the noble blacksmith that he almost appeared in person, as the story advanced. "I don't know what he had done to rile up Mars Gardner, but all of us knew that the Blacksmith was going to be flogged. When the whippers from Mississippi got to the plantation. The blacksmith worked on day and night. All day he was shoein horses and all the spare time he had he was makin a knife. When the whippers got there all of us were brought out to watch the whippin but the blacksmith, Jim Gardner did not wait to feel the lash, he jumped right into the bunch of overseers and negro whippers and knifed two whippers and one overseer to death; then stuck the sharp knife into his arm and bled to death."

Suicide seemed the only hope for this man of strength. He could not humble himself to the brutal ordeal of being beaten by the slave whippers.

"When the war started, we kept hearing about the soldiers and finally they set up their camp in the forest near us. The corn was ready to bring into the barn and the soldiers told Mr. Mooney to let the slaves gather it and put it into the barns. Some of the soldiers helped gather and crib the corn. I wanted to help but Miss Puss was afraid they would press me into service and made me hide in the cellar. There was a big keg of apple cider in the cellar and every day Miss Puss handed down a big plate of fresh ginger snaps right out of the oven, so I was well fixed." The old man remembers that after the corn was in the crib the soldiers turned in their horses to eat what had fallen to the ground.

Before the soldiers became encamped at the Mooney plantation they had camped upon a hill and some skirmishing had occurred. Uncle Joe remembers the skirmish and seeing cannon balls come over the fields. The cannon balls were chained together and the slave children would run after the missils. Sometimes the chains would cut down trees as the balls rolled through the forest.

"Do you believe in witchcraft?" was asked while interviewing the aged negro. "No" was the answer. "I had a cousin that was a full blooded Indian and a Voodoo doctor. He got me to help him with his Voodoo work. A lot of people both white and black sent for the Indian when they were sick. I told him I would do the best I could, if it would help sick people to get well. A woman was sick with rhumatism and he was going to see her. He sent me into the woods to dig up poke roots to boil. He then took the brew to the house where the sick woman lived. Had her to put both feet in a tub filled with warm water, into which he had placed the poke root brew. He told the woman she had lizards in her body and he was going to bring them out of her. He covered the woman with a heavy blanket and made her sit for a long time, possibly an hour, with her feet in the tub of poke root brew and water. He had me slip a good many lizards into the tub and when the woman removed her feet, there were the lizards. She was soon well and believed the lizards had come out of her legs. I was disgusted and would not practice with my cousin again."

"So you didn't fight in the Civil War," was asked Uncle Joe.

"Of course I did, when I got old enough I entered the service and barbacued meat until the war closed." Barbacueing had been Uncle Joe's specialty during slavery days and he followed the same profession during his service with the federal army. He was freed by the emancuapation proclamation, and soon met and married Sadie Scott, former Slave of Mr. Scott, a Tennessee planter. Sadie only lived a short time after her marriage. He later married Amy Doolins. Her father was named Carmuel. He was a blacksmith and after he was free, the countrymen were after him to take his life. He was shot nine times and finally killed himself to prevent meeting death at the hands of the clansmen.

Joseph William Carter is a cripple. In 1933 he fell and broke his right thigh-bone and since that time he has walked with a crutch. He stays up quite a lot and is always glad to welcome visitors. He possesses a noble character and is admired by his friends and neighbors. Tall, straight, lean of body, his nose is aquiline; these physical characteristics he inherited from his Indian ancestors. His gentle nature, wit, and good humor are characteristics handed to him by his mother and fostered by the gentle rearing of his southern mistress.

When Uncle Joe Carter celebrated the 100dth aniversary of his birth a large cake was presented to him, decorated with 100 candles. The party was attended by children and grandchildren, friends and neighbors. "What is your political viewpoint?" was asked the old man.

"My politics is my love for my country". "I vote for the man, not the party."

Uncle Joe's religion is the religion of decency and virtue. "I don't want to be hard in my judgement," said he, "But I wish the whole world would be decent. When I was a young man, women wore more clothes in bed than they now wear on the street."

"Papa has always been a lover of horses but he does not care for Automobiles nor aeroplanes," said a daughter of Uncle Joe. Uncle Joe has seven daughters, he says they have always been obedient and attentive to their parents. Their mother passed away seven years ago. The sons and daughters of Uncle Joe remember their grand-mother and recall stories recounted by her of her captivity among the Indians.

"Papa had no gray hairs until after mama died. His hair turned gray from grief at her loss," said Mrs. Della Smith, one of his daughters. Uncle Joe's smile reveals a set of unusually sound teeth from which only one tooth is missing.

Like all fathers and grandfathers, Uncle Joe recounts the cute deeds and funny sayings of the little children he has been associated with: how his own children with feather bedecked crowns enacted the capture of their grandmother and often played "Voo-Doo Doctor."

Uncle Joe stresses the value of work, not the enforced labor of the slave but the cheerful toil of free people. He is glad that his sons and daughters are industrious citizens and is proud they maintain clean homes for their families. He is happy because his children have never known bondage, and he respects the laws of his country and appreciates the interest that the citizens of Evansville have always showed in the negro race.

After Uncle Joe became a young man he met many Indians from the tribe that had held his mother captive. Through them he learned much about his father which his mother had never told him.

Though he was a Gardner slave and would have been Joseph Gardner, he took the name of Carter from a step father and is known as Joseph Carter.

United States. Work Projects Administration

Grace Monroe
Dist. 4
Jefferson County

SLAVE STORY
OHIO COUNTY EX-SLAVE, MRS. ELLEN CAVE, RELATES HER
EXPERIENCES

MRS. ELLEN CAVE

Assistant editor of "The Rising Sun Recorder" furnished the following story which had appeared in the paper, March 19, 1937.

Mrs. Cave was in slavery for twelve years before she was freed by the Emancipation Proclamation. When she gave her story to Aubrey Robinson she was living in a temporary garage home back of the Rising Sun courthouse having lost everything in the 1937 flood.

Mrs. Cave was born on a plantation in Taylor County Kentucky. She was the property of a man who did not live up to the popular idea of a Southern gentleman, whose slaves refused to leave them, even after their freedom was declared.

When she was a year old her mother was sold to someone in Louisana and she did not see her again until 1867, when they were re-united in Carrolton, Kentucky. Her father died when she was a baby.

Mrs. Cave told of seeing wagon loads of slaves sold down the river. She, herself was put on the block several times but never actually sold, although she would have preferred being sold rather than the continuation of the ordeal of the block.

Her master was a "mean man" who drank heavily, he had twenty slaves that he fed now and then, and gave her her freedom after the war only when she would remain silent about it no longer. He was a Southern sympathiser but joined the Union army where he became a captain and was in charge of a Union commissary. Finally he was suspected and charged with mustering supplies to the rebels. He was imprisoned for some time, then court-martialed and sentenced to die. He escaped by bribing his negro guard.

Mrs. Cave said that her master's father had many young women slaves and sold his own half-breed children down the river to Louisiana plantations where the work was so severe that the slaves soon died.

While in slavery, Mrs. Cave worked as a maid in the house until she grew older when she was forced to do all kinds of outdoor labor. She remembered sawing logs in the snow all day. In the summer she pitched hay or any other man's work in the field. She was trained to carry three buckets of water at the same time, two in her hands and one on her head and said she could still do it.

On this plantation the chief article of food for the slaves was bran-bread, although the master's children were kind and often slipped them out meat or other food.

Mrs. Cave remembered seeing General Woolford and General Morgan of the Southern forces when they made friendly visits to the plantation. She saw General Grant twice during the war. She saw soldiers drilling near the plantation. Later she was caught and whipped by night riders, or "pat-a-rollers", as she tried to slip out to negro religious meetings.

Mrs. Cave was driven from her plantation two years after the war and came to Carrollton [TR: earlier, Carrolton] Kentucky, where she found her mother and soon married James Cave, a former slave on a plantation near hers in Taylor county. Mrs. Cave had thirteen children.

For many years Mrs. Cave has lived on a farm about two and one half mi. south of Rising Sun. Everything she had was washed away in the flood and she lived in the court house garage until her home could be rebuilt.

Federal Writers' Project
of the W.P.A.
District #8
Marion County
Anna Pritchett
1200 Kentucky Avenue

FOLKLORE
MRS. HARRIET CHEATAM—EX-SLAVE
816 Darnell Street

MRS. HARRIET CHEATAM

Interviewer's Comment

ncidents in the life of Mrs. Cheatam as she told them to me.

Interview

"I was born, in 1843, in Gallatin, Tennessee, 94 years ago this coming (1937) Christmas day."

"Our master, Martin Henley, a farmer, was hard on us slaves, but we were happy in spite of our lack."

"When I was a child, I didn't have it as hard as some of the children in the quarters. I always stayed in the "big house," slept on the floor, right near the fireplace, with one quilt for my bed and one quilt to cover me. Then when I growed up, I was in the quarters."

"After the Civil war, I went to Ohio to cook for General Payne. We had a nice life in the general's house."

"I remember one night, way back before the Civil war, we wanted a goose. I went out to steal one as that was the only way we slaves would have one. I crept very quiet-like, put my hand in where they was and grabbed, and what do you suppose I had? A great big pole cat. Well, I dropped him quick, went back, took off all my clothes, dug a hole, and buried them. The next night I went to the right place, grabbed me a nice big goose, held his neck and feet so he couldn't holler, put him under my arm, and ran with him, and did we eat?"

"We often had prayer meeting out in the quarters, and to keep the folks in the "big house" from hearing us, we would take pots, turn them down, put something under them, that let the sound go in the pots, put them in a row by the door, then our voices would not go out, and we could sing and pray to our heart's content."

"At Thanksgiving time we would have pound cake. That was fine. We would take our hands and beat and beat our cake dough, put the dough in a skillet, cover it with the lid and put it in the fireplace. (The covered skillet would act our ovens of today.) It would take all day to bake, but it sure would be good; not like the cakes you have today."

"When we cooked our regular meals, we would put our food in pots, slide them on an iron rod that hooked into the fireplace. (They were called pot hooks.) The pots hung right over the open fire and would boil until the food was done."

"We often made ash cake. (That is made of biscuit dough.) When the dough was ready, we swept a clean place on the floor of the fireplace, smoothed the dough out with our hands, took some ashes, put them on top of the dough, then put some hot coals on top of the ashes, and just left it. When it was done, we brushed off the coals, took out the bread, brushed off the ashes, child, that was bread."

"When we roasted a chicken, we got it all nice and clean, stuffed him with dressing, greased him all over good, put a cabbage leaf on the floor of the fireplace, put the chicken on the cabbage leaf, then covered him good with another cabbage leaf, and put hot coals all over and around him, and left him to roast. That is the best way to cook chicken."

Mrs. Cheatam lives with a daughter, Mrs. Jones. She is a very small old lady, pleasant to talk with, has a very happy disposition. Her eyes, as she said, "have gotten very dim," and she can't piece her quilts anymore. That was the way she spent her spare time.

Interviewer's Comment

She has beautiful white hair and is very proud of it.

Submitted December 1, 1937
Indianapolis, Indiana

United States. Work Projects Administration

Ex-Slave stories
District #5
Vanderburgh County
Lauana Creel

JAMES CHILDRESS' STORY
312 S.E. Fifth Street, Evansville, Indiana

JAMES CHILDRES

From an interview with James Childress and from John Bell both living at 312 S.E. Fifth Street, Evansville, Indiana.

Known as Uncle Jimmy by the many children that cluster about the aged man never tiring of his stories of "When I was chile."

"When I was a chile my daddy and mamma was slaves and I was a slave," so begins many recounted tales of the long ago.

Born at Nashville, Tennessee in the year 1860, Uncle Jimmie remembers the Civil War with the exciting events as related to his own family and the family of James Childress, his master. He remembers sorrow expressed in parting tears when "Uncle Johnie and Uncle Bob started to war." He recalls happy days when the beautiful valley of the Cumberland was abloom with wild flowers and fertile acres were carpeted with blue grass.

"A beautiful view could always be enjoyed from the hillsides and there were many pretty homes belonging to the rich citizens. Slaves kept the lawns smooth and tended the flowers for miles around Nashville, when I was a child," said Uncle Jimmie.

Uncle Jimmie Childress has no knowledge of his master's having practiced cruelty towards any slave. "We was all well fed, well clothed and lived in good cabins. I never got a cross word from Mars John in my life," he declared. "When the slaves got their freedom they rejoiced staying up many nights to sing, dance and enjoy themselves, although they still depended on old Mars John for food and bed, they felt too excited to work in the fields or care for the stock. They hated to leave their homes but Mr. Childress told them to go out and make homes for themselves."

"Mother got work as a housekeeper and kept us all together. Uncle Bob got home from the War and we lived well enough. I have lived at Evansville since 1881, have worked for a good many men and John Bell will tell you I have had only friends in the city of Evansville."

Uncle Jimmie recalls how the slaves always prayed to God for freedom and the negro preachers always preached about the day when the slaves would be no longer slaves but free and happy.

"My people loved God, they sang sacred songs, 'Swing Low Sweet Charriot' was one of the best songs they knew". Here uncle Jimmie sang a stanza of the song and said it related to God's setting the negroes free.

"The negroes at Mr. Childress' place were allowed to learn as much as they could. Several of the young men could read and write. Our master was a good man and did no harm to anybody."

James Childress is a black man, small of stature, with crisp wooly dark hair. He is glad he is not mulatto but a thorough blooded negro.

United States. Work Projects Administration

Federal Writers' Project
of the W.P.A.
District #6
Marion County
Anna Pritchett
1200 Kentucky Avenue

FOLKLORE
MRS. SARAH COLBERT—EX-SLAVE
1505 North Capitol Avenue, Indianapolis, Indiana

MRS. SARAH COLBERT

Mrs. Sarah Carpenter Colbert was born in Allen County, Kentucky in 1855. She was owned by Leige Carpenter, a farmer.

Her father, Isaac Carpenter was the grandson of his master, Leige Carpenter, who was very kind to him. Isaac worked on the farm until the old master's death. He was then sold to Jim McFarland in Frankfort Kentucky. Jim's wife was very mean to the slaves, whipped them regularly every morning to start the day right.

One morning after a severe beating, Isaac met an old slave, who asked him why he let his mistress beat him so much. Isaac laughed and asked him what he could do about it. The old man told him if he would bite her foot, the next time she knocked him down, she would stop beating him and perhaps sell him.

The next morning he was getting his regular beating, he willingly fell to the floor, grabbed his mistress' foot, bit her very hard. She tried very hard to pull away from him, he held on still biting, she ran around in the room, Isaac still holding on. Finally, she stopped beating him and never attempted to strike him again.

The next week he was put on the block, being a very good worker and a very strong man, the bids were high.

His young master, Leige Jr., outbid everyone and bought him for $1200.00.

His young mistress was very mean to him. He went again to his old friend for advice. This time he told him to get some yellow dust, sprinkle it around in his mistress' room and if possible, got some in her shoes. This he did and in a short time he was sold again to Johnson Carpenter in the same county. He was not really treated any better there. By this time he was very tired of being mistreated. He remembered his old master telling him to never let anyone be mean to him. He ran away to his old mistress, told her of his many hardships, and told her what the old master had told him, so she sent him back. At the next sale she bought him, and he lived there until slavery was abolished.

Her grandfather, Bat Carpenter, was an ambitious slave; he dug ore and bought his freedom, then bought his wife by paying $50.00 a year to her master for her. She continued to work on the farm of her own master for a very small wage.

Bat's wife, Matilda, lived on the farm not far from him, he was allowed to visit her every Sunday. One Sunday, it looked like rain, his master told him to gather in the oats, he refused to do this and was beaten with a raw hide. He was so angry, he went to one of the witch-crafters for a charm so he could fix his old master.

The witch doctor told him to get five new nails, as there were five members in his master's family, walk to the barn, then walk backwards a few steps, pound one nail in the ground, giving each nail the name of each member of the family, starting with the master, then the mistress, and so on through the family. Each time one nail was pounded down in the ground, walk backwards and nail the next one in until all were pounded deep in the ground. He did as instructed and was never beaten again.

Jane Garmen was the village witch. She disturbed the slaves with her cat. Always at milking time the cat would appear, and at night would go from one cabin to another, putting out the grease lamps with his paw. No matter how they tried to kill the cat, it just could not be done.

An old witch doctor told them to melt a dime, form a bullet with the silver, and shoot the cat. He said a lead bullet would never kill a bewitched animal. The silver bullet fixed the cat.

Jane also bewitched the chickens. They were dying so fast anything they did seemed useless. Finally a big fire was built and the dead chickens thrown into the fire, that burned the charm, and no more chickens died.

Interviewer's Comment

Mrs. Colbert lives with her daughter in a very comfortable home. She seems very happy and was glad to talk of her early days. How she would laugh when telling of the experiences of her family.

She has reared a large family of her own, and feels very proud of them.

Submitted December 1, 1937
Indianapolis, Indiana

Wm. R. Mays
Dist. 4
Johnson County, Ind.
July 29, 1937

SLAVERY DAYS OF MANDY COOPER OF LINCOLN COUNTY, KENTUCKY
FRANK COOPER
715 Ott St., Franklin, Ind.

FRANK COOPER

rank Cooper, an aged colored man of Franklin, relates some very interesting conditions that existed in slavery days as handed down to him by his mother.

Mandy Cooper, the mother of Frank Cooper, was 115 years old when she died; she was owned by three different families: the Good's, the Burton's, and the Cooper's, all of Lincoln Co. Kentucky.

"Well, Ah reckon Ah am one of the oldest colored men hereabouts," confessed aged Frank Cooper. "What did you all want to see me about?" My mission being stated, he related one of the strangest categories alluding to his mother's slave life that I have ever heard.

"One day while mah mammy was washing her back my sistah noticed ugly disfiguring scars on it. Inquiring about them, we found, much to our amazement, that they were mammy's relics of the now gone, if not forgotten, slave days.

"This was her first reference to her "misery days" that she had evah made in my presence. Of course we all thought she was tellin' us a big story and we made fun of her. With eyes flashin', she stopped bathing, dried her back and reached for the smelly ole black whip that hung behind the kitchen door. Biddin' us to strip down to our waists, my little mammy with the boney bent-ovah back, struck each of us as hard as evah she could with that black-snake whip, each stroke of the whip drew blood from our backs. "Now", she said to us, "you have a taste of slavery days." With three of her children now having tasted of some of her "misery days" she was in the mood to tell us more of her sufferings; still indelibly impressed in my mind. [TR: illegible handwritten note here.]

'My ole back is bent ovah from the quick-tempered blows feld by the red-headed Miss Burton.

'At dinner time one day when the churnin' wasn't finished for the noonday meal', she said with an angry look that must have been reborn in mah mammy's eyes—eyes that were dimmed by years and hard livin', 'three white women beat me from anger because they had no butter for their biscuits and cornbread. Miss Burton used a heavy board while the missus used a whip. While I was on my knees beggin' them to quit, Miss Burton hit the small of mah back with the heavy board. Ah knew no more until kind Mr. Hamilton, who was staying with the white folks, brought me inside the cabin and brought me around with the camphor bottle. Ah'll always thank him—God bless him—he picked me up where they had left me like a dog to die in the blazin' noonday sun.

'After mah back was broken it was doubted whether ah would evah be able to work again or not. Ah was placed on the auction block to be bidded for so mah own-er could see if ah was worth anything or not. One man bid $1700 after puttin' two dirty fingahs in my mouth to see my teeth. Ah bit him and his face showed angah. He then wanted to own me so he could punish me.

'Thinkin' his bid of $1700 was official he unstrapped his buggy whip to beat me, but my mastah saved me. My master declared the bid unofficial.

'At this auction my sister was sold for $1900 and was never seen by us again.'

"My mother related some experiences she had with the Paddy-Rollers, later called the "Kuklux", these Pad-dy-Rollers were a constant dread to the Negroes. They would whip the poor darkeys unmercifully without any cause. One night while the Negroes were gathering for a big party and dance they got wind of the approaching Paddy-Rollers in large numbers on horseback. The Negro men did not know what to do for protection, they became desperate and decided to gather a quantity of grapevines and tied them fast at a dark place in the road. When the Paddy-Rollers came thundering down the road bent on deviltry and unaware of the trap set for them, plunged head-on into these strong grapevines and three of their number were killed and a score was badly injured. Sever-al horses had to be shot following injuries.

"When the news of this happening spread it was many months before the Paddy-Rollers were again heard of."

Albert Strope, Field Worker
Federal Writers' Project
St. Joseph County—District #1
Mishawaka, Indiana

EX-SLAVE
REV. H.H. EDMUNDS
403 West Hickory Street
Elkhart, Indiana

H.H. EDMUNDS

Rev. H.H. Edmunds has resided at 403 West Hickory Street in Elkhart for the past ten years. Born in Lynchburg, Virginia, in 1859, he lived there for several years. Later he was taken to Mississippi by his master, and finally to Nashville, Tennessee, where he lived until his removal to Elkhart.

Mr. Edmunds is very religious, and for many years has served his people as a minister of the Gospel. He feels deeply that the religion of today has greatly changed from the "old time religion." In slavery days, the colored people were so subjugated and uneducated that he claims they were especially susceptible to religion, and poured out their religious feelings in the so-called negro spirituals. Mr. Edmunds is convinced that the superstitions of the colored people and their belief in ghosts and gobblins is due to the fact that their emotions were worked upon by slave drivers to keep them in subjugation. Oftentimes white people dressed as ghosts, frightened the colored people into doing many things under protest. The "ghosts" were feared far more than the slave-drivers.

The War of the Rebellion is not remembered by Mr. Edmunds, but he clearly remembers the period following the war known as the Reconstruction Period. The Negroes were very happy when they learned they were free as a result of the war. A few took advantage of their freedom immediately, but many, not knowing what else to do, remained with their former masters. Some remained on the plantations five years after they were free. Gradually they learned to care for themselves, often through instructions received from their former masters, and then they were glad to start out in the world for themselves. Of course, there were exceptions, for the slaves who had been abused by cruel masters were only too glad to leave their former homes.

The following reminiscense is told by Mr. Edmunds:

"As a boy, I worked in Virginia for my master, a Mr. Farmer[TR:?]. He had two sons who served as bosses on the farm. An elder sister was the head boss. After the war was over, the sister called the colored people together and told them that they were no longer slaves, that they might leave if they wished.

"The slaves had been watering cucumbers which had been planted around barrels filled with soil. Holes had been bored in the barrels, and when water was poured in the barrels, it gradually seeped out through the holes thus watering the cucumbers.

"After the speech, one son told the slaves to resume their work. Since I was free, I refused to do so, and as a result, I received a terrible kicking. I mentally resolved to get even some day. Years afterward, I went to the home of this man for the express purpose of seeking revenge. However, I was received so kindly, and treated so well, that all thoughts of vengeance vanished. For years after, my former boss and I visited each other in our own homes."

Mr. Edmunds states that the Negro people prefer to be referred to as colored people, and deeply resent the name "nigger."

United States. Work Projects Administration

Archie Koritz, Field Worker
Federal Writers' Project
Lake County—District #1
Gary, Indiana

EX-SLAVES
JOHN EUBANKS & FAMILY
Gary, Indiana

JOHN EUBANKS & FAMILY

Gary's only surviving Civil War veteran was born a slave in Barren County, Kentucky, June 6, 1836. His father was a mulatto and a free negro. His mother was a slave on the Everrett plantation and his grandparents ware full-blooded African negroes. As a child he began work as soon as possible and was put to work hoeing and picking cotton and any other odd jobs that would keep him busy. He was one of a family of several children, and is the sole survivor, a brother living in Indianapolis, having died there in 1935.

Following the custom of the south, when the children of the Everrett family grew up, they married and slaves were given them for wedding presents. John was given to a daughter who married a man of the name of Eubanks, hence his name, John Eubanks. John was one of the more fortunate slaves in that his mistress and master were kind and they were in a state divided on the question of slavery. They favored the north. The rest of the children were given to other members of the Everrett family upon their marriage or sold down the river and never saw one another until after the close of the Civil War.

Shortly after the beginning of the Civil War, when the north seemed to be losing, someone conceived the idea of forming negro regiments and as an inducement to the slaves, they offered them freedom if they would join the Union forces. John's mistress and master told him that if he wished to join the Union forces, he had their consent and would not have to run away like other slaves were doing. At the beginning of the war, John was twenty-one years of age. When Lincoln freed the slaves by his Emancipation Proclamation, John was promptly given his freedom by his master and mistress.

John decided to join the northern army which was located at Bowling Green, Kentucky, a distance of thirty-five miles from Glasgow where John was living. He had to walk the entire thirty-five miles. Although he fails to remember all the units that he was attached to, he does remember that it was part of General Sherman's army. His regiment started with Sherman on his famous march through Georgia, but for some reason unknown to John, shortly after the campaign was on its way, his regiment was recalled and sent elsewhere.

His regiment was near Vicksburg, Mississippi, at the time Lee surrendered. Since Lee was a proud southerner and did not want the negroes present when he surrendered, Grant probably for this reason as much as any other refused to accept Lee's sword. When Lee surrendered there was much shouting among the troops and John was one of many put to work loading cannons on boats to be shipped up the river. His company returned on the steamboat "Indiana." Upon his return to Glasgow, [HW:

Ky.] he saw for the first time in six years, his mother and other members of his family who had returned free.

Shortly after he returned to Glasgow at the close of the Civil War, he saw several colored people walking down the highway and was attracted to a young colored girl in the group who was wearing a yellow dress. Immediately he said to himself, "If she ain't married there goes my wife." Sometime later they met and were married Christmas day in 1866. To this union twelve children were born four of whom are living today, two in Gary and the others in the south. After his marriage he lived on a farm near Glasgow for several years, later moving to Louisville, where he worked in a lumber yeard. He came to Gary in 1924, two years after the death of his wife.

President Grant was the first president for whom he cast his vote and he continued to vote until old age prevented him from walking to the polls.

Although Lincoln is one of his favorite heroes, Teddy Roosevelt tops his list of great men and he never failed to vote for him.

In 1926, he was the only one of three surviving memebers of the Grand Army of the Republic in Gary and mighty proud of the fact that he was the only one in the parade. In 1937 he is the sole survivor.

He served in the army as a member of Company K of the 108th, Kentucky Infantry (Negro Volunteers).

When General Morgan, the famous southern raider, crossed the Ohio on his raid across southern Indiana, John was one of the Negro fighters who after heavy fighting, forced Morgan to recross the river and retreat back to the south. He also participated in several skirmishes with the cavalry troops commanded by the famous Nathan Bedfored Forrest, and was a member of the Negro garrison at Fort Pillow, on the Mississippi which was assaulted and captured. This resulted in a massacre of the negro soldiers. John was in several other fights, but as he says, "never onct got a skinhurt."

At the present time, Mr. Eubanks is residing with his daughter, Mrs. Bertha Sloss and several grandchildren, in Gary, Indiana. He is badly crippled with rheumatism, has poor eyesight and his memory is failing. Otherwise his health is good. Most of his teeth are good and they are a source of wonder to his dentist. He is ninety-eight years of age and his wish in life now, is to live to be a hundred. Since his brother and mother both died at ninety-eight and his paternal grandfather at one hundred-ten years of age, he has a good chance to realize this ambition.

Because of his condition most of this interview was had from his grandchildren, who have taken notes in recent years of any incidents that he relates. He is proud that most of his fifty grandchildren are high school graduates and that two are attending the University of Chicago.

In 1935, he enjoyed a motor trip, when his family took him back to Glasgow for a visit. He suffered no ill effects from the trip.

Archie Koritz, Field Worker
816 Mound Street, Valparaiso, Indiana
Federal Writers' Project
Lake County, District #1
Gary, Indiana

EX-SLAVES
INTERVIEW WITH JOHN EUBANKS, EX-SLAVE

JOHN EUBANKS

John Eubanks, Gary's only negro Civil War survivor has lived to see the ninety-eighth anniversary of his birth and despite his advanced age, recalls with surprising clarity many interesting and sad events of his boyhood days when a slave on the Everett plantation.

He was born in Glasgow, Barron County, Kentucky, June 6, 1839, one of seven children of a chattel of the Everett family.

The old man retains most of his faculties, but bears the mark of his extreme age in an obvious feebleness and failing sight and memory. He is physically large, says he once was a husky, weighing over two hundred pounds, bears no scars or deformities and despite the hardships and deprivations of his youth, presents a kindly and tolerant attitude.

"I remembah well, us young uns on the Everett plantation," he relates, "I worked since I can remembah, hoein', pickin' cotton and othah chohs 'round the fahm. We didden have much clothes, nevah no undahweah, no shoes, old ovahalls and a tattahed shirt, wintah and summah. Come de wintah, it be so cold mah feet weah plumb numb mos' o' de time and manya time—when we git a chanct—we druve the hogs from outin the bogs an' put ouah feet in the wahmed wet mud. They was cracked and the skin on the bottoms and in de toes weah cracked and bleedin' mos' o' time, wit bloody scabs but de summah healed them agin."

"Does yohall remembah, Granpap," his daughter prompted, "Yoh mahstah—did he treat you mean?"

"No," his tolerant acceptance apparent in his answer, "it weah done thataway. Slaves weah whipt and punished and the younguns belonged to the mahstah to work foah him oh to sell. When I weah 'bout six yeahs old, Mahstah Everett give me to Tony Eubanks as a weddin' present when he married mahstah's daughtah Becky. Becky would'n let Tony whip her slaves who came from her fathah's plantation. 'They ah my prophty,' she say, 'an' you caint whip dem.' Tony whipt his othah slaves but not Becky's."

"I remembah" he continued, "how they tied de slave 'round a post, wit hands tied togedder 'round the post, then a husky lash his back wid a snakeskin lash 'til hisn back were cut and bloodened, the blood spattered" gesticulating with his unusually large hands, "an' hisn back all cut up. Den they'd pouh salt watah on hem. Dat dry and hahden and stick to hem. He nevah take it off 'till it heal. Sometimes I see marhstah Everett hang a slave tip-toe. He tie him up so he stan' tip-toe an' leave him thataway.

"I be twenty-one wehn wah broke out. Mahstah Eubanks say to me, 'Yohall don' need to run 'way ifn yo-hall want to jine up wid de ahmy.' He say, 'Deh would be a fine effin slaves run off. Yohall don' haf to run off, go right on and I do not pay dat fine.' He say, "nlist in de ahmy but don' run off.' Now I walk thirty-five mile from Glasgow to Bowling Green to dis place—to da 'nlistin' place—from home fouh mile—to Glasgow—to Bowling Green, thirty-five mile. On de road I meet up with two boys, so we go on. Dey run 'way from Kentucky, and we go together. Then some Bushwackers come down de road. We's scared and run to the woods and hid. As we run tru de woods, pretty soon we heerd chickens crowing. We fill ouah pockets wit stones. We goin' to kill chickens to eat. Pretty soon we heerd a man holler, 'You come 'round outta der'—and I see a white man and come out. He say, 'What yoh all doin' heah?' I turn 'round and say, 'well boys, come on boys,' an' the boys come out. The man say, 'I'm Union Soldier. What yoh all doin' heah?' I say, 'We goin' to 'nlist in de ahmy.' He say, 'Dat's fine' and he say, 'come 'long' He say, 'git right on white man's side'—we go to station. Den he say, 'You go right down to de station and give yoh inforhmation. We keep on walkin'. Den we come to a white house wit stone steps in front so we go in. An' we got to 'nlistin' place and jine up wit de ahmy.

"Den we go trainin' in d' camp and we move on. Come to a little town ... a little town. We come to Bolling Green ... den to Louiville. We come to a rivah ... a rivah (painfully recalling) d' Mississippi.

"We weah 'nfantry and petty soon we gits in plenty fights, but not a scratch hit me. We chase dem cavalry. We run dem all night and next mohnin' d' Captain he say, 'Dey done broke down.' When we rest, he say 'See dey don' trick you.' I say, 'We got all d' ahmy men togedder. We hold dem back 'til help come.'

"We don' have no tents. Sleep on naked groun' in wet and cold and rain. Mos' d' time we's hungry but we win d' war and Mahstah Eubanks tell us we no moah hisn property, we's free now."

The old man can talk only in short sentences and his voice dies to a whisper and soon the strain became evident. He was tired. What he does remember is with surprising clearness especially small details, but with a helpless gesture, he dismisses names and locations. He remembers the exact date of his discharge, March 20, 1866, which his daughter verified by producing his discharge papers. He remembers the place, Vicksburg, the Company—K, and the Regiment, 180th. Dropping back once more to his childhood he spoke of an incident which his daughter says makes them all cry when he relates it, although they have heard it many times.

"Mahstah Everett whipt me onct and mothah she cried. Then Mahstah Everett say, 'Why yoh all cry?—Yoh cry I whip anothah of these young uns. She try to stop. He whipt 'nother. He say, 'Ifn yoh all don' stop, yoh be whipt too!' and mothah she trien to stop but teahs roll out, so Mahstah Everett whip her too.

"I wanted to visit mothah when I belong to Mahst' Eubanks, but Becky say, 'Yoh all best not see youh mothah, or yoh wan' to go all de time' then explaining, 'she wan' me to fohgit mothah, but I nevah could. When I cm back from d' ahmy, I go home to mothah and say 'don' y'know me?' She say, 'No, I don' know you.' I say, 'Yoh don' know me?' She say, 'No, ah don' know yoh.' I say,

'I'se John.' Den she cry and say how ahd growd and she thought I'se daid dis long time. I done 'splain how the many fights I'se in wit no scratch and she bein' happy."

Speaking of Abraham Lincoln's death, he remarked, "Sho now, ah remembah dat well. We all feelin' sad and all d'soldiers had wreaths on der guns."

Upon his return from the army he married a young negress he had seen some time previous at which time he had vowed some day to make her his wife. He was married Christmas day, 1866. For a number of years he lived on a farm of his own near Glasgow. Later he moved with his family to Louisville where he worked in a lumber yard. In 1923, two years after the death of his wife, he came to Gary, when he retired. He is now living with his daughter, Mrs. Sloss, 2713 Harrison Boulevard, Gary.

United States. Work Projects Administration

Cecil C. Miller
Dist. #3
Tippecanoe Co.

INTERVIEW WITH MR. JOHN W. FIELDS, EX-SLAVE OF CIVIL WAR
PERIOD
September 17, 1937

MR. JOHN W. FIELDS

John W. Fields, 2120 North Twentieth Street, Lafayette, Indiana, now employed as a domestic by
Judge Burnett is a typical example of a fine colored
gentleman, who, despite his lowly birth and adverse circumstances, has labored and economized until he has
acquired a respected place in his home community. He
is the owner of three properties; un-mortgaged, and is

a member of the colored Baptist Church of Lafayette. As will later be seen his life has been one of constant effort to better himself spiritually and physically. He is a fine example of a man who has lived a morally and physically clean life. But, as for his life, I will let Mr. Fields speak for himself:

"My name is John W. Fields and I'm eighty-nine (89) years old. I was born March 27, 1848 in Owensburg, Ky. That's 115 miles below Louisville, Ky. There was 11 other children besides myself in my family. When I was six years old, all of us children were taken from my parents, because my master died and his estate had to be settled. We slaves were divided by this method. Three disinterested persons were chosen to come to the plantation and together they wrote the names of the different heirs on a few slips of paper. These slips were put in a hat and passed among us slaves. Each one took a slip and the name on the slip was the new owner. I happened to draw the name of a relative of my master who was a widow. I can't describe the heartbreak and horror of that separation. I was only six years old and it was the last time I ever saw my mother for longer than one night. Twelve children taken from my mother in one day. Five sisters and two brothers went to Charleston, Virginia, one brother and one sister went to Lexington Ky., one sister went to Hartford, Ky., and one brother and myself stayed in Owensburg, Ky. My mother was later allowed to visit among us children for one week of each year, so she could only remain a short time at each place.

"My life prior to that time was filled with heart-aches and despair. We arose from four to five O'clock in the morning and parents and children were given hard work, lasting until nightfall gaves us our respite. After a meager supper, we generally talked until we grew sleepy, we had to go to bed. Some of us would read, if we were lucky enough to know how.

"In most of us colored folks was the great desire to able to read and write. We took advantage of every opportunity to educate ourselves. The greater part of the plantation owners were very harsh if we were caught trying to learn or write. It was the law that if a white man was caught trying to educate a negro slave, he was liable to prosecution entailing a fine of fifty dollars and a jail sentence. We were never allowed to go to town and it was not until after I ran away that I knew that they sold anything but slaves, tobacco and wiskey. Our ignorance was the greatest hold the South had on us. We knew we could run away, but what then? An offender guilty of this crime was subjected to very harsh punishment.

"When my masters estate had been settled, I was to go with the widowed relative to her place, she swung me up on her horse behind her and promised me all manner of sweet things if I would come peacefully. I didn't fully realise what was happening, and before I knew it, I was on my way to my new home. Upon arrival her manner changed very much, and she took me down to where there was a bunch of men burning brush. She said, "see those men" I said: yes. Well, go help them, she replied. So at the age of six I started my life as an independent slave. From then on my life as a slave was a repetition of hard work, poor quarters and board. We had no beds at that time, we just "bunked" on the floor. I had one blanket and manys the night I sat by the fireplace during the long cold nights in the winter.

"My Mistress had separated me from all my family but one brother with sweet words, but that pose was dropped after she reached her place. Shortly after I had been there, she married a northern man by the name of David Hill. At first he was very nice to us, but he gradually acquired a mean and overbearing manner toward us, I remember one incident that I don't like to remember. One of the women slaves had been very sick and she was unable to work just as fast as he thought she ought to. He had driven her all day with no results. That night after completeing our work he called us all together. He made me hold a light, while he whipped her and then made one of the slaves pour salt water on her bleeding back. My innerds turn yet at that sight.

"At the beginning of the Civil War I was still at this place as a slave. It looked at the first of the war as if the south would win, as most of the big battles were won by the South. This was because we slaves stayed at home and tended the farms and kept their families.

"To eliminate this solid support of the South, the Emancipation Act was passed, freeing all slaves. Most of the slaves were so ignorant they did not realize they were free. The planters knew this and as Kentucky never seceeded from the Union, they would send slaves into Kentucky from other states in the south and hire them out to plantations. For these reasons I did not realize that I was free untill 1864. I immediately resolved to run away and join the Union Army and so my brother and I went to Owensburg, Ky. and tried to join. My brother was taken, but I was refused as being too young. I [HW: tried] at Evansville, Terre Haute and Indianapolis but was unable to get in. I then tried to find work and was finally hired by a man at $7.00 a month. That was my first independent job. From then on I went from one job to another working as general laborer.

"I married at 24 years of age and had four children. My wife has been dead for 12 years and 8 months. Mr. Miller, always remember that:

"The brightest man, the prettiest flower
May be cut down, and withered in an hour."

"Today, I am the only surviving member who helped organize the second Baptist Church here in Lafayette, 64 years ago. I've tried to live according to the way the Lord would wish, God Bless you."

"The clock of Life is wound but once.
Today is yours, tomorrow is not.
No one knows when the hands will stop."

Cecil Miller
Dist. #3
Tipp. Co. [TR: Tippecanoe Co.]

NEGRO FOLKLORE
MR. JOHN FIELDS, EX-SLAVE
2120 N. 20th St. Lafayette, Indiana

MR. JOHN FIELDS

M r. Fields says that all negro slaves were ardent believers in ghosts, supernatual powers, tokens and "signs." The following story illustrates the point.

"A turkey gobbler had mysteriously disappeared from one of the neighboring plantations and the local slaves were accused of commeting the fowl to a boiling pot. A slave convicted of theft was punished severly. As all of the slaves denied any knowledge of the turkey's whereabouts, they were instructed to make a search of the entire plantation."

"On one part of the place there was a large peach orchard. At the time the trees were full of the green fruit. Under one of the trees there was a large cabinet or "safe" as they were called. One of the slaves accidently opened the safe and, Behold, there was Mr. Gobbler peacefully seated on a number of green peaches.

"The negro immediately ran back and notified his master of the discovery. The master returned to the orchard with the slave to find that the negro's wild tale was true. A turkey gobbler sitting on a nest of green peaches. A bad omen.

"The master had a son who had been seriously injured some time before by a runaway team, and a few days after this unusual occurence with the turkey, the son died. After his death, the word of the turkey's nesting venture and the death of the master's son spread to this four winds, and for some time after this story was related wherever there was a public gathering with the white people or the slave population."

All through the south a horseshoe was considered an omen of good luck. Rare indeed was the southern home that did not have one nailed over the door. This insured the household and all who entered of plesant prospects while within the home. If while in the home you should perhaps get into a violent argument, never hit the other party with a broom as it was a sure indication of bad luck.

If Grandad had the rheumatics, he would be sure of relief if he carried a buckeye in his pocket.

Of all the Ten Commandments, the one broken most by the negro was: Thou Shalt Not Steal This was due mostly to the insufficent food the slaves obtained. Most of the planters expected a chicken to suddenly get heavenly aspirations once in a while, but as Mr. Fields says, "When a beautiful 250 pound hog suddenly tries to kidnap himself, the planter decided to investigate." It occured like this:

A 250 pound hog had been fruitless. The planter was certain that the culprit was among his group of slaves, so he decided to personally conduct a quiet investigation.

One night shortly after the moon had risen in the sky, two of the negroes were seated at a table in one of the cabins talking of the experiences of the day. A knock sounded on the door. Both slaves jumped up and cautiously peeked out of the window. Lo there was the master patiently waiting for an answer. The visiting negro decided that the master must not see both of them and he asked the other to conceal him while the master was there. The other slave told him to climb into the attic and be perfectly quiet. When this was done, the tenant of the cabin answered the door.

The master strode in and gazed about the cabin. He then turned abruptly to the slave and growled, 'Alright, where is that hog you stoled.' 'Massa, replied the negro, 'I know nothing about no hog. The master was certain that the slave was lying and told him so in no uncertain terms. The terrified slave said, 'Massa, I know nothing of any hog. I never seed him. The Good Man up above knows

I never seed him. HE knows every thing and HE knows I didn't steal him; The man in the attic by this time was aroused at the misunderstood conversation taking place below him. Disregarding all, he raised his voice and yelled, 'He's a liar, Massa, he knows just as much about it as I do.'

Most of the strictly negro folklore has faded into the past. The younger negro generations who have been reared and educated in the north have lost this bearing and assumed the lore of the local white population through their daily contact with the whites. The older negro natives of this section are for the most part employed as domestics and through this channel rapidly assimilated the employers viewpoint in most of his beliefs and conversations.

Ex-Slave Stories
District 5
Vanderburgh County
Lauana Creel

INDIANS MADE SLAVES AMONG THE NEGROES.
INTERVIEWS WITH GEORGE FORTMAN
Cor. Bellemeade Ave. and Garvin St.
Evansville, Indiana, and other interested citizens

GEORGE FORTMAN

"The story of my life, I will tell to you with sincerest respect to all and love to many, although reviewing the dark trail of my childhood and early youth causes me great pain." So spoke George Fortman, an aged man and former slave, although the history of his life reveals that no Negro blood runs through his veins.

"My story necessarily begins by relating events which occurred in 1838, when hundreds of Indians were rounded up like cattle and driven away from the valley of the Wabash. It is a well known fact recorded in the histories of Indiana that the long journey from the beautiful Wabash Valley was a horrible experience for the fleeing Indians, but I have the tradition as relating to my own family, and from this enforced flight ensued the tragedy of my birth."

The aged ex-slave reviews tradition. "My two ancestors, John Hawk, a Blackhawk Indian brave, and Racheal, a Chackatau maiden had made themselves a home such as only Indians know, understand and enjoy. He was a hunter and a fighter but had professed faith in Christ through the influence of the missionaries. My greatgrandmother passed the facts on to her children and they have been handed down for four generations. I, in turn, have given the traditions to my children and grandchildren.

"No more peaceful home had ever offered itself to the red man than the beautiful valley of the Wabash river. Giant elms, sycamores and maple trees bordered the stream while the fertile valley was traversed with creeks and rills, furnishing water in abundance for use of the Indian campers.

"The Indians and the white settlers in the valley transacted business with each other and were friendly towards each other, as I have been told by my mother, Eliza, and my grandmother, Courtney Hawk.

"The missionaries often called the Indian families together for the purpose of teaching them and the Indians had been invited, prior to being driven from the valley, to a sort of festival in the woods. They had prepared much food for the occasion. The braves had gone on a long hunt to provide meat and the squaws had prepared much corn and other grain to be used at the feast. All the tribes had been invited to a council and the poor people were happy, not knowing they were being deceived.

"The decoy worked, for while the Indians were worshiping God the meeting was rudely interrupted by orders of the Governor of the State. The Governor, whose duty it was to give protection to the poor souls, caused them to be taken captives and driven away at the point of swords and guns.

"In vain, my grandmother said, the Indians prayed to be let return to their homes. Instead of being given their liberty, some several hundred horses and ponies were captured to be used in transporting the Indians away from the valley. Many of the aged Indians and many innocent children died on the long journey and traditional stories speak of that journey as the 'trail of death.'"

"After long weeks of flight, when the homes of the Indians had been reduced to ashes, the long trail still carried them away from their beautiful valley. My great-grandfather and his squaw became acquainted with a party of Indians that were going to the canebrakes of Alabama. The pilgrims were not well fed or well clothed and they were glad to travel towards the south, believing the climate would be favorable to their health.

"After a long and dreary journey, the Indians reached Alabama. Rachael had her youngest papoose strapped on to her back while John had cared for the larger child, Lucy. Sometimes she had walked beside her father but often she had become weary or sleepy and he had carried her many miles of the journey, besides the weight of blankets and food. An older daughter, Courtney, also accompanied her parents.

"When they neared the cane lands they heard the songs of Negro slaves as they toiled in the cane. Soon they were in sight of the slave quarters of Patent George's plantation. The Negroes made the Indians welcome and the slave dealer allowed them to occupy the cane house; thus the Indians became slaves of Patent George.

"Worn out from his long journey John Hawk became too ill to work in the sugar cane. The kindly-disposed

Negroes helped care for the sick man but he lived only a few months. Rachel and her two children remained on the plantation, working with the other slaves. She had nowhere to go. No home to call her own. She had automatically become a slave. Her children had become chattel.

"So passed a year away, then unhappiness came to the Indian mother, for her daughter, Courtney, became the mother of young Master Ford George's child. The parents called the little half-breed "Eliza" and were very fond of her. The widow of John Hawk became the mother of Patent George's son, Patent Junior.

"The tradition of the family states that in spite of these irregular occurrences the people at the George's southern plantation were prosperous, happy, and lived in peace each with the others. Patent George wearied of the Southern climate and brought his slaves into Kentucky where their ability and strength would amass a fortune for the master in the iron ore regions of Kentucky.

"With the wagon trains of Patent and Ford George came Rachel Hawk and her daughters, Courtney, Lucy and Rachel. Rachel died on the journey from Alabama but the remaining full blooded Indians entered Kentucky as slaves.

"The slave men soon became skilled workers in the Hillman Rolling Mills. Mr. Trigg was owner of the vast iron works called the "Chimneys" in the region, but listed as the Hillman, Dixon, Boyer, Kelley and Lyons Furnaces. For more than a half century these chimneys smoked as the most valuable development in the western area of Kentucky. Operated in 1810, these furnaces had refined iron ore to supply the United States Navy with cannon balls and grape shot, and the iron smelting industry continued until after the close of the Civil War.

"No slaves were beaten at the George's plantation and old Mistress Hester Lam allowed no slave to be sold. She was a devoted friend to all.

"As Eliza George, daughter of Ford George and Courtney Hawk, grew into young womanhood the young master Ford George went oftener and oftener to social functions. He was admired for his skill with firearms and for his horsemanship. While Courtney and his child remained at the plantation Ford enjoyed the companship of the beautiful women of the vicinity. At last he brought home the beautiful Loraine, his young bride. Courtney was stoical as only an Indian can be. She showed no hurt but helped Mistress Hester and Mistress Loraine with the house work."

Here George Fortman paused to let his blinded eyes look back into the long ago. Then he again continued with his story of the dark trail.

"Mistress Loraine became mother of two sons and a daughter and the big white two-story house facing the Cumberland River at Smith Landing, Kentucky, became a place of laughter and happy occasions, so my mother told me many times.

"Suddenly sorrow settled down over the home and the laughter turned into wailing, for Ford George's body was found pierced through the heart and the half-breed, Eliza, was nowhere to be found.

"The young master's body lay in state many days.

Friends and neighbors came bringing flowers. His mother, bowed with grief, looked on the still face of her son and understood—understood why death had come and why Eliza had gone away.

"The beautiful home on the Cumberland river with its more than 600 acres of productive land was put into the hands of an administrator of estates to be readjusted in the interest of the George heirs. It was only then Mistress Hester went to Aunt Lucy and demanded of her to tell where Eliza could be found.

'She has gone to Alabama, Ole Mistus', said Aunt Lucy, 'Eliza was scared to stay here.' A party of searchers were sent out to look for Eliza. They found her secreted in a cane brake in the low lands of Alabama nursing her baby boy at her breast. They took Eliza and the baby back to Kentucky. I am that baby, that child of unsatisfactory birth."

The face of George Fortman registered sorrow and pain, it had been hard for him to retell the story of the dark road to strange ears.

"My white uncles had told Mistress Hester that if Eliza brought me back they were going to build a fire and put me in it, my birth was so unsatisfactory to all of them, but Mistress Hester always did what she believed was right and I was brought up by my own mother.

"We lived in a cabin at the slave quarters and mother worked in the broom cane. Mistress Hester named me Ford George, in derision, but remained my friend. She was never angry with my mother. She knew a slave had to submit to her master and besides Eliza did not know she was Master Ford George's daughter."

The truth had been told at last. The master was both the father of Eliza and the father of Eliza's son.

"Mistress Hester believed I would be feeble either in mind or body because of my unsatisfactory birth, but I developed as other children did and was well treated by Mistress Hester, Mistress Lorainne and her children.

"Master Patent George died and Mistress Hester married Mr. Lam, while slaves kept working at the rolling mills and amassing greater wealth for the George families.

"Five years before the outbreak of the Civil War Mistress Hester called all the slaves together and gave us our freedom. Courtney, my grandmother, kept house for Mistress Lorainne and wanted to stay on, so I too was kept at the George home. There was a sincere friendship as great as the tie of blood between the white family and the slaves. My mother married a negro ex-slave of Ford George and bore children for him. Her health failed and when Mistress Puss, the only daughter of Mistress Lorainne, learned she was ill she persuaded the Negro man to sell his property and bring Eliza back to live with her."

[TR: in following section the name George 'Fordman' is used twice.]

"Why are you called George Fordman when your name is Ford George?" was the question asked the old man.

"Then the Freedsmen started teaching school in Kentucky the census taker called to enlist me as a pupil. 'What do you call this child?' he asked Mistress Lorainne. 'We call him the Little Captain because he carried himself like a soldier,' said Mistress Lorainne. 'He is the son of my husband and a slave woman but we are rearing him.' Mistress Lorainne told the stranger that I had been named Ford George in derision and he suggested she list me in the census as George Fordsman, which she did, but she never allowed me to attend the Freedmen's School, desiring to keep me with her own children and let me be taught at home. My mother's half brother, Patent George allowed his name to be reversed to George Patent when he enlisted in the Union Service at the outbreak of the Civil War."

Some customs prevalent in the earlier days were described by George Fordman. "It was customary to conduct a funeral differently than it is conducted now," he said. "I remember I was only six years old when old Mistress Hester Lam passed on to her eternal rest. She was kept out of her grave several days in order to allow time for the relatives, friends and ex-slaves to be notified of her death.

"The house and yard were full of grieving friends. Finally the lengthy procession started to the graveyard. Within the George's parlors there had been Bible passages read, prayers offered up and hymns sung, now the casket was placed in a wagon drawn by two horses. The casket was covered with flowers while the family and friends rode in ox carts, horse-drawn wagons, horseback, and with still many on foot they made their way towards the river.

"When we reached the river there were many canoes busy putting the people across, besides the ferry boat was in use to ferry vehicles over the stream. The ex-slaves were crying and praying and telling how good granny had been to all of them and explaining how they knew she had gone straight to Heaven, because she was so kind—and a Christian. There were not nearly enough boats to take the crowd across if they crossed back and forth all day, so my mother, Eliza, improvised a boat or 'gunnel', as the craft was called, by placing a wooden soap box on top of a long pole, then she pulled off her shoes and, taking two of us small children in her arms, she paddled with her feet and put us safely across the stream. We crossed directly above Iaka, Livingston county, three miles below Grand River.

"At the burying ground a great crowd had assembled from the neighborhood across the river and there were more songs and prayers and much weeping. The casket was let down into the grave without the lid being put on and everybody walked up and looked into the grave at the face of the dead woman. They called it the 'last look' and everybody dropped flowers on Mistress Hester as they passed by. A man then went down and nailed on the lid and the earth was thrown in with shovels. The ex-slaves filled in the grave, taking turns with the shovel. Some of the men had worked at the smelting furnaces so long that their hands were twisted and hardened from con-tact with the heat. Their shoulders were warped and their bodies twisted but they were strong as iron men from their years of toil. When the funeral was over mother put us across the river on the gunnel and we went home, all missing Mistress Hester.

"My cousin worked at Princeton, Kentucky, making shoes. He had never been notified that he was free by the kind emancipation Mrs. Hester had given to her slaves, and he came loaded with money to give to his white folks. Mistress Lorainne told him it was his own money to keep or to use, as he had been a free man several months.

"As our people, white and black and Indians, sat talking they related how they had been warned of approaching trouble. Jack said the dogs had been howling around the place for many nights and that always presaged a death in the family. Jack had been compelled to take off his shoes and turn them soles up near the hearth to prevent the howling of the dogs. Uncle Robert told how he believed some of Mistress Hester's enemies had planted a shrub near her door and planted it with a curse so that when the shrub bloomed the old woman passed away. Then another man told how a friend had been seen carrying a spade into his cousin's cabin and the cousin had said, 'Daniel, what foh you brung that weapon into by [TR: my?] cabin? That very spade will dig my grave,' and sure enough the cousin had died and the same spade had been used in digging his grave.

"How my childish nature quailed at hearing the superstitions discussed, I cannot explain. I have never believed in witchcraft nor spells, but I remember my Indian grandmother predicted a long, cold winter when she noticed the pelts of the coons and other furred creatures were exceedingly heavy. When the breastbones of the fowls were strong and hard to sever with the knife it was a sign of a hard, cold and snowy winter. Another superstition was this: 'A green winter, a new graveyard—a white winter, a green graveyard.'"

George Fortman relates how, when he accompanied two of his cousins into the lowlands—there were very many Katy-dids in the trees—their voices formed a nerve-racking orchestra and his cousin told him to tip-toe to the trees and touch each tree with the tips of his fingers. This he did, and for the rest of the day there was quiet in the forest.

"More than any other superstition entertained by the slave Negroes, the most harmful was the belief on conjurors. One old Negro woman boiled a bunch of leaves in an iron pot, boiled it with a curse and scattered the tea therein brewed, and firmly believed she was bringing destruction to her enemies. 'Wherever that tea is poured there will be toil and troubles,' said the old woman.

"The religion of many slaves was mostly superstition. They feared to break the Sabbath, feared to violate any of the Commandments, believing that the wrath of God would follow immediately, blasting their lives.

"Things changed at the George homestead as they change everywhere," said George Fortman. "When the Civil War broke out many slaves enlisted in hopes of receiving freedom. The George Negroes were already free but many thought it their duty to enlist and fight for the emancipation of their fellow slaves. My mother took her family and moved away from the plantation and worked in the broom cane. Soon she discovered she could not make enough to rear her children and we were turned over to the court to be bound out.

"I was bound out to David Varnell in Livingston County by order of Judge Busch and I stayed there until I was fifteen years of age. My sister learned that I was unhappy there and wanted to see my mother, so she influenced James Wilson to take me into his home. Soon goodhearted Jimmy Wilson took me to see Mother and I went often to see her."

Sometimes George would become stubborn and hard to control and then Mr. Wilson administered chastisement. His wife could not bear to have the boy punished. 'Don't hit him, Jimmie, don't kick him,' would say the good Scotch woman, who was childless. 'If he does not obey me I will whip him,' James Wilson would answer. So the boy learned the lesson of obedience from the old couple and learned many lessons in thrift through their examples.

"In 1883 I left the Wilson home and began working and trying to save some money. River trade was prosperous and I became a 'Roustabout'. The life of the roustabout varied some with the habits of the roustabout and the disposition of the mate. We played cards, shot dice and talked to the girls who always met the boats. The 'Whistling Coon' was a popular song with the boatmen and one version of 'Dixie Land'. One song we often sang when near a port was worded 'Hear the trumpet Sound'—

Hear the trumpet sound,
Stand up and don't sit down,
Keep steppin' 'round and 'round,
Come jine this elegant band.

If you don't step up and jine the bout,
Old Missus sure will fine it out,
She'll chop you in the head wid a golen ax,
You never will have to pay da tax,
Come jine the roust-a-bout band."

From roust-a-bout George became a cabin boy, cook, pilot, and held a number of positions on boats, plowing different streams. There was much wild game to be had and the hunting season was always open. He also remembers many wolves, wild turkeys, catamounts and deer in abundance near the Grand River. "Pet deer loafed around the milking pens and ate the feed from the mangers" said he.

George Fortman is a professor of faith in Christ. He was baptized in Concord Lake, seven miles from Clarksville, Tennessee, became a member of the Pleasant Greene Church at Callwell, Kentucky and later a member of the Liberty Baptist Church at Evansville.

"I have always kept in touch with my white folks, the George family," said the man, now feeble and blind. "Four years ago Mistress Puss died and I was sent for but was not well enough to make the trip home."

Too young to fight in the Civil War, George was among those who watched the work go on. "I lived at Smiths Landing and remember the battle at Fort Donnelson. It was twelve miles away and a long cinder walk reached from the fort for nearly thirty miles. The cinders were brought from the iron ore mills and my mother and I have walked the length of it many times." Still reviewing the long, dark trail he continued. "Boatloads of soldiers passed Smith's Landing by day and night and the reports of cannon could be heard when battles were fought. We children collected Munnie balls near the fort for a long time after the war."

Although the George family never sold slaves or separated Negro families, George Fortman has seen many boats loaded with slaves on the way to slave marts. Some of the George Negroes were employed as pilots on the boats. He also remembers slave sales where Negroes were auctioned by auctioneers, the Negroes stripped of clothes to exhibit their physique.

"I have always been befriended by three races of people, the Caucassian, the African, and the Negro," declares George Fortman. "I have worked as a farmer, a river man, and been employed by the Illinois Central Railroad Company and in every position I have held I have made loyal friends of my fellow workmen." One friend, treasured in the memory of the aged ex-slave is Ollie James, who once defended George in court.

George Fortman has friends at Dauson Springs, Grayson Springs, and other Kentucky resorts. He has been a citizen of Evansville for thirty-five years and has had business connections here for sixty-two years. He janitored for eleven years for the Lockyear Business College, but his days of usefulness are over. He now occupies a room at Bellemeade Ave. and Garvin St. and his only exercise consists of a stroll over to the Lincoln High School. There he enjoys listening to the voices of the pupils as they play about the campus. "They are free", he rejoices. "They can build their own destinies, they did not arrive in this life by births of unsatisfactory circumstances. They have the world before them and my grandsons and granddaughters are among them."

Federal Writers' Project
of the W.P.A.
District #6
Marion County
Anna Pritchett
1200 Kentucky Avenue

FOLKLORE
JOHN HENRY GIBSON—EX-SLAVE
Colton Street

JOHN HENRY GIBSON

John Henry Gibson was born a slave, many years ago, in Scott County, N.C.

His old master, John Henry Bidding, was a wealthy farmer; he also owned the hotel, or rooming house.

When court was in session the "higher ups" would come to this house, and stay until the court affairs were settled.

Mr. Bidding, who was very kind to his slaves, died when John Gibson was very young. All slaves and other property passed on to the son, Joseph Bidding, who in turn was as kind as his father had been.

Gibson's father belonged to General Lee Gibson, who was a neighboring farmer. He saw and met Miss Elizabeth Bidding's maid; they liked each other so very much, Miss Elizabeth bought him from General Gibson, and let him have her maid as his wife. The wife lived only a short time, leaving a little boy.

After the Civil war, a white man, by the name of Luster, was comming to Ohio, brought John Gibson with him. They came to Indianapolis, and Gibson liked it so well, he decided to remain; Mr. Luster told him if he ever became dissatisfied to come on to Ohio to him, but he remained in Indianapolis until 1872, then went back south, married, came back, and made Indianapolis his home.

Interviewer's Comment

Mr. Gibson is very old, but does not know his exact age. He fought in the Civil war, and said he could not be very young to have done that.

His sight is very nearly gone, can only distinguish light and dark.

He is very proud of his name, having been named for his old master.

Submitted January 24, 1938
Indianapolis, Indiana

Submitted by:
William Webb Tuttle
District No. 2
Muncie, Indiana

NEGRO SLAVES IN DELAWARE COUNTY
MRS. BETTY GUWN
MRS. HATTIE CASH, DAUGHTER,
residing at 1101 East Second Street
Muncie, Indiana

MRS. BETTY GUWN

Mrs. Betty Guwn was born March 25, 1832, as a slave on a tobacco plantation, near Canton, Kentucky. It was a large plantation whose second largest product was corn. She was married while quite young by the slave method which was a form of union customary between the white masters. If the contracting parties were of different plantations the masters of the two estates bargained and the one sold his rights to the one on whose plantation they would live. Her master bought her husband, brought him and set them up a shack. Betty was the personal attendant of the Mistress. The home was a large Colonial mansion and her duties were many and responsible. However, when her house duties were caught up her mistress sent her immediately to the fields. Discipline was quite stern there and she was "lined up" with the others on several occasions.

Her cabin home began to fill up with children, fifteen in all. The ventilation was ample and the husband would shoot a prowling dog from any of the four sides of the room without opening the door. The cracks between the logs would be used by cats who could step in anywhere. The slaves had "meetin'" some nights and her mistress would call her and have her turn a tub against her mansion door to keep out the sound.

Her master was very wealthy. He owned and managed a cotton farm of two thousand acres down in Mississippi, not far from New Orleans. Once a year he spent three months there gathering and marketing his cotton. When he got ready to go there he would call all his slaves about him and give them a chance to volunteer. They had heard awful tales of the slave auction block at New Orleans, and the Master would solemnly promise them that they should not be sold if they went down of their own accord. "My Mistress called me to her and privately told me that when I was asked that question I should say to him: "I will go". The Master had to take much money with him and was afraid of robbers. The day they were to start my Mistress took me into a private room and had me remove most of my clothing; she then opened a strong box and took out a great roll of money in bills; these she strapped to me in tight bundles, arranging them around my waist in the circle of my body. She put plenty of dresses over this belt and when she was through I wore a bustle of money clear around my belt. I made a funny "figger" but no one noticed my odd shape because I was a slave and no one expected a slave to "know better". We always got through safely and I went down with my Mistress every year. Of course my husband stayed at home to see after the family, and took them to the fields when too young to work under the task master, or over-seer. Three months was a long time to be separated."

"When the Civil War came on there was great excitement among we slaves. We were watched sharply, especially soldier timber for either army. My husband ran away early and helped Grant to take Fort Donaldson. He said he would free himself, which he did; but when we were finally set free all our family prepared to leave. The Master begged us to stay and offered us five pounds of meal and two pounds of pork jowl each week if we would stay and work. We all went to Burgard, Kentucky, to live. At that time I was about 34 years old. My husband has been dead a long time and I live with my children. If the "Good Lord" spares me until next March the 25th, I will be 106 years old. I walk all about lively without crutches and eye-glasses and I have never been sick until this year when a tooth gave me trouble; but I had it pulled."

Archie Koritz, Field Worker
Federal Writers' Project
Porter County—District #1
Valparaiso, Indiana

EX-SLAVES
MRS. HOCKADAY
2581 Madison Street
Gary, Indiana

MRS. HOCKADAY

Mrs. Hockaday is the daughter of an ex-slave and like so many others does not care to discuss the dark side of slavery and the cruel treatment that some of them received.

After the Civil War the slaves who for the most part were unskilled and ignorant, found it very difficult to adjust themselves to their new life as free persons. Formerly, they lived on the land of their masters and although compelled to work long hours, their food and lodging were provided for them. After their emancipation, this life was changed. They were free and had to think for themselves and make a living. Times for the negro then was much the same as during the depression. Several of the slaves started out to secure jobs, but all found it difficult to adjust themselves to the new life and difficult to secure employment. Many came back to their old owners and many were afraid to leave and continued on much as before.

The north set up stores or relief stations where the

negro who was unable to secure employment could ob-
tain food and shelter. Mrs. Hockaday says it was the same
as conditions have been the last few years.

About all the negro was skilled at was servant work
and when they came north, they encountered the same
difficulties as several of the colored folks who, driven by
the terrible living conditions in the south four years ago,
came to Gary. Arriving here they believed they were capa-
ble of servant work. However they were not accustomed
to modern appliances and found it very difficult to adjust
themselves. It was the same after the Emancipation.

Many owners were kind and religious and had schools
for their slaves, where they could learn to read and write.
These slaves were more successful in securing employment.

Although the negro loved the Bible most of all books,
and were mostly Methodists and Baptists, their different religious beliefs is caused by the slave owners having
churches for the slaves. Whatever church the master belonged to, the slaves belonged to, and continued in the
same church after the war.

Since slaves took the name of their owners, children in
the same family would have different names. Mr. Hockaday's father and his brothers and sisters all had different
names. On the plantation they were called "Jones' Jim,"
"Brown's Jones," etc. Many on being freed left their old
homes and adopted any name that they took a fancy to.
One slave that Mrs. Hockaday remembers took the name
of Green Johnson and says he often remarked that he
surely was green to adopt such a name. His grandson

in Gary is an exact double for Clark Gable, except he is brown, and Gable is white.

Many slave owners gave their slaves small tracts of land which they could tend after working hours. Anything raised belonged to them and they could even sell the products and the money was theirs. Many slaves were able to save enough from these tracts to purchase their freedom long before the Emancipation.

Another condition that confronted the negro in the north was that they were not understood like they were by the southern people. In the south they were trusted and considered trustworthy by their owners. Even during the Civil War, they were trusted with the family jewels, silver, etc., when the northern army came marching by, whereas in the north, even though they freed the slaves, they would not trust them. For that reason, many of the slaves did not like the northern people and remained or returned to the southern plantations.

The slave owners thought that slavery was right and nothing was wrong about selling and buying human beings if they were colored, much as a person would purchase a horse or automobile today. The owners who whipped their slaves usually stripped them to the waist and lashed them with a long leather whip, commonly called a blacksnake.

Mrs. Hockaday is a large, pleasant, middle-aged woman and does not like to discuss the cruel side of slavery and only recalls in a general way what she had heard old slaves discuss.

Federal Writers' Project
of the W.P.A.
District #6
Marion County
Anna Pritchett
1200 Kentucky Avenue

FOLKLORE
ROBERT HOWARD—EX-SLAVE
1840 Boulevard Place

ROBERT HOWARD

Robert Howard, an ex-slave, was born in 1852, in Clara County, Kentucky.

His master, Chelton Howard, was very kind to him.

The mother, with her five children, lived on the Howard farm in peace and harmony.

His father, Beverly Howard, was owned by Bill Anderson, who kept a saloon on the river front.

Beverly was "hired out" in the house of Bill Anderson. He was allowed to go to the Howard farm every Saturday night to visit with his wife and children. This visit was always looked forward to with great joy, as they were devoted to the father.

The Howard family was sold only once, being owned first by Dr. Page in Henry County, Kentucky. The family was not separated; the entire family was bought and kept together until slavery was abolished.

Interviewer's Comment

Mr. Howard seems to be a very kind old man, lives in the house for aged colored people (The Alpha Home).

He has no relatives, except a brother. He seems well satisfied living in the home.

Submitted January 10, 1938
Indianapolis, Indiana

Grace Monroe
Dist. 4
Jefferson County

SLAVE STORY
MR. MATTHEW HUME, A FORMER SLAVE

MATTHEW HUME

M r. Hume had many interesting experiences to tell concerning the part slavery had played in his family. On the whole they were fortunate in having a good master who would not keep an overseer who whipped his "blacks".

His father, Luke Hume, lived in Trimble County Kentucky and was allowed to raise for himself one acre of tobacco, one acre of corn, garden stuff, chickens and have the milk and butter from one cow. He was advised to save his money by the overseer, but always drank it up. On this plantation all the slaves were free from Saturday noon until Monday morning and on Christmas and the Fourth of July. A majority of them would go to Bedford or Milton and drink, gamble and fight. On the neighboring farm the slaves were treated cruelly. Mr. Hume had a brother-in-law, Steve Lewis, who carried marks on his back. For years he had a sore that would not heal where his master had struck him with a blacksnake whip.

Three good overseers were Jake Mack and Mr. Crafton, Mr. Daniel Payne was the owner who asked his people to report any mistreatment to him. He expected obe-dience however.

When Mr. Hume was a small boy he was placed in the fields to hoe. He also wanted a new implement. He was so small he was unable to keep near enough to the men and boys to hear what they were talking about, he remembered bringing up the rear one day, when he saw a large rock he carefully covered it with dirt, then came down hard on it breaking his hoe. He missed a whipping and received a new tool to replace the old one, after this he could keep near enough to hear what the other workers were talking about.

Another of his duties was to go for the cattle, he had to walk around the road about a mile, but was permitted to come back through the fields about a quarter of a mile. One afternoon his mistress told him to bring a load of wood when he came in. In the summer it was the custom to have the children carry the wood from the fields. When he came up he saw his mistress was angry this peeved him, so that he stalked into the hall and slammed his wood into the box. About this time his mistress shoved him into a small closet and locked the door. He made such a howl that he brought his mother and father to the rescue and was soon released from his prison.

As soon as the children were old enough they were placed in the fields to prepare the ground for setting to-bacco plants. This was a very complicated procedure. The ground was made into hills, each requiring about four feet of soil. The child had to get all the clods broken fine. Then place his foot in the center and leave his track. The plants were to be set out in the center and woe to the youngster who had failed to pulverize his hill. After one plowing the tobacco was hand tended. It was long green and divided into two grades. It was pressed by being placed in large hogsheads and weighted down. On one occasion they were told their tobacco was so eaten up that the worms were sitting on the fence waiting for the leaves to grow but nevertheless in some manner his master hid the defects and received the best price paid in the community.

The mistress on a neighboring plantation was a devout Catholic, and had all the children come each Sunday after-noon to study the catechism and repeat the Lord's Prayer. She was not very successful in training them in the Catholic faith as when they grew up most of them were either Baptists or Methodists. Mr. Hume said she did a lot of good in leading them to Christ but he did not learn much of the catechism as he only attended for the treat. After the service they always had candy or a cup of sugar.

On the Preston place there was a big strapping negro of eighteen whom the overseer attempted to whip receiving the worst of it. He then went to Mr. Hume's owner and asked for help but was told he would have to seek elsewhere for help. Finally some one was found to assist. Smith was tied to a tree and severely beaten, then they were afraid to untie him, when the overseer finally ventured up and loosened the ropes, Smith kicked him as hard as he could and ran to the Payne estate refusing to return. He was a good helper here where he received kind treatment.

A bad overseer was discharged once by Mr. Payne because of his cruelty to Mr. Luke Hume. The corncrib was a tiny affair where a man had to climb out one leg at a time, one morning just as Mr. Hume's father was climbing out with his feed, he was struck over the head with a large club, the next morning he broke the scoop off an iron shovel and fastened the iron handle to his body. This time he swung himself from the door of the crib and seeing the overseer hiding to strik him he threw his bar, which made a wound on the man's head which did not knock him out. As soon as Mr. Payne heard of the disturbance the overseer was discharged and Mr. Mack placed in charge of the slaves.

One way of exacting obedience was to threaten to send offenders South to work in the fields. The slaves around Lexington, Kentucky, came out ahead on one occasion. The collector was Shrader. He had the slaves handcuffed to a large leg chain and forced on a flat boat. There were so many that the boat was grounded, so some of the slaves were released to push the boat off. Among the "blacks" was one who could read and write. Before Shrader could chain them up again, he was seized and chained, taken to below Memphis Tennessee and forced to work in the cotton fields until he was able to get word from Richmond identifying him. In the meantime the educated negro issued freedom papers to his companions. Many of them came back to Lexington, Kentucky where they were employed.

Mr. Hume thought the Emancipation Proclamation was the greatest work that Abraham Lincoln ever did. The colored people on his plantation did not learn of it until the following August. Then Mr. Payne and his sons offered to let them live on their ground with conditions similar to our renting system, giving a share of the crop. They remained here until Jan. 1, 1865 when they crossed the Ohio at Madison. They had a cow which had been given them before the Emancipation Proclamation was issued but this was taken away from them. So they came to Ind. homeless, friendless and penniless.

Mr. Hume and his aged wife have been married 62 years and resided in the same community for 55 years where they are highly respected by all their neighbors.

He could not understand the attitude of his race who preferred to remain in slavery receiving only food and shelter, rather than to be free citizens where they could have the right to develop their individualism.

Virginia Tulley
District #2
Fort Wayne, Indiana

EX-SLAVE OF ALLEN COUNTY
[MRS. HENRIETTA JACKSON]

References:
A. Ft. Wayne News Sentinel November 21, 1931
B. Personal interview
[TR: There are no 'A' and 'B' annotations in the inter-
view.]

HENRIETTA JACKSON

Mrs. Henrietta Jackson, Fort Wayne resident, is distinguished for two reasons; she is a centen-narian and an ex-slave. Residing with her daughter, Mrs. Jackson is very active and helps her daughter, who operates a restaurant, do some of the lighter work. At the time I called, an August afternoon of over 90 degrees temperature, Mrs. Jackson was busy sweeping the floor. A little, rather stooped, shrunken body, Mrs. Jackson gets around slowly but without the aid of a cane or support of any kind. She wears a long dark cotton dress with a bandana on her head with is now quite gray. Her skin is walnut brown her eyes peering brightly through the wrinkles. She is intelligent, alert, cordial, very much interested in all that goes on about her.

Just how old Mrs. Jackson is, she herself doesn't know, but she thinks she is about 105 years old. She looks much younger. Her youngest child is 73 and she had nine, two of whom were twins. Born a slave in Virginia, record of her birth was kept by the master. She cannot remember her father as he was soon sold after Mrs. Jackson's death [TR: birth?]. When still a child she was taken from her mother and sold. She remembers the auction block and that she brought a good price as she was strong and healthy. Her new master, Tom Robinson, treated her well and never beat her. At first she was a plough hand, working in the cotton fields, but then she was taken into the house to be a maid. While there the Civil War broke out. Mrs. Jackson remembers the excitement and the coming and going. Gradually the family lost its wealth, the home was broken up. Everything was destroyed by the armies. Then came freedom for the slaves. But Mrs. Jackson stayed on with the master for awhile. After leaving she went to Alabama where she obtained work in a laundry "ironing white folks' collars and cuffs." Then she got married and in 1917 she came to live with her daughter in Fort Wayne. Her husband, Levy Jackson, has been dead 50 years. Of her children, only two are left. Mrs. Jackson is sometimes very lonesome for her old home in "Alabamy", where her friends lived, but for the most part, she is happy and contented.

Federal Writers' Project
of the W.P.A.
District #6
Marion County
Anna Pritchett
1200 Kentucky Avenue

FOLKLORE
MRS. LIZZIE JOHNSON
706 North Senate Avenue, Apt. 1

LIZZIE JOHNSON

Mrs. Johnson's father, Arthur Locklear, was born in Wilmington, N.C. in 1822. He lived in the South and endured many hardships until 1852. He was very fortunate in having a white man befriend him in many ways. This man taught him to read and write. Many nights after a hard days work, he would lie on the floor in front of the fireplace, trying to study by the light from the blazing wood, so he might improve his reading and writing.

He married very young, and as his family increased, he became ambitious for them. Knowing their future would be very dark if they remained South.

He then started a movement to come north. There were about twenty-six or twenty-eight men and women, who had the same thoughts about their children, banded together, and in 1852 they started for somewhere, North.

The people selected, had to be loyal to the cause of

their children's future lives, morally clean, truthful, and hard-working.

Some had oxen, some had carts. They pooled all of their scant belongings, and started on their long hard journey.

The women and children rode in the ox-carts, the men walked. They would travel a few days, then stop on the roadside to rest. The women would wash their few clothes, cook enough food to last a few days more, then they would start out again. They were six weeks making the trip.

Some settled in Madison, Indiana. Two brothers and their families went on to Ohio, and the rest came to Indianapolis.

John Scott, one of their number was a hod carrier. He earned $2.50 a day, knowing that would not accumulate fast enough, he was strong and thrifty. After he had worked hard all day, he would spend his evenings putting new bottoms in chairs, and knitting gloves for anyone who wanted that kind of work. In the summer he made a garden, sold his vegetables. He worked very hard, day and night, and was able to save some money.

He could not read or write, but he taught his children the value of truthfulness, cleanliness of mind and body, loyalty, and thrift. The father and his sons all worked together and bought some ground, built a little house where the family lived many years.

Before old Mr. Scott died, he had saved enough money to give each son $200.00. His bank was tin cans hidden around in his house.

Will Scott, the artist, is a grandson of this John Scott.

The thing these early settlers wanted most, was for their children to learn to read and write. So many of them had been caught trying to learn to write, and had had their thumbs mashed, so they would not be able to hold a pencil.

Interviewer's Comment

Mrs. Johnson is a very interesting old woman and remembers so well the things her parents told her. She deplores the "loose living," as she calls it of this generation.

She is very deliberate, but seems very sure of the story of her early life.

Submitted December 9, 1937
Indianapolis, Indiana

Ex-Slave Stories
District No. 5
Vanderburgh County
Lauana Creel

THE STORY OF BETTY JONES
429 Oak Street, Evansville, Ind.

BETTY JONES

From an Interview with Elizabeth Jones at 429 Oak Street, Evansville, Ind.

"Yes Honey, I was a slave, I was born at Henderson, Kentucky and my mother was born there. We belonged to old Mars John Alvis. Our home was on Alvis's Hill and a long plank walk had been built from the bank of the Ohio river to the Alvis home. We all liked the long plank walk and the big house on top of the hill was a pretty place."

Betty Jones said her master was a rich man and had made his money by raising and selling slaves. She only recalls two house servants were mulatoes. All the other slaves were black as they could be.

Betty Alvis lived with her parents in a cabin near her master's home on the hill. She recalls no unkind treatment. "Our only sorrow was when a crowd of our slave friends would be sold off, then the mothers, brothers, sisters, and friends always cried a lot and we children would grieve to see the grief of our parents."

The mother of Betty was a slave of John Alvis and married a slave of her master. The family lived at the slave quarters and were never parted. "Mother kept us all together until we got set free after the war," declares Betty. Many of the Alvis negroes decided to make their homes at Henderson, Kentucky. "It was a nice town and work was plentiful."

Betty Alvis was brought to Evansville by her parents. The climate did not agree with the mother so she went to Princeton, Kentucky to live with her married daughter and died there.

Betty Alvis married John R. Jones, a native of Tennessee, a former slave of John Jones, a Tennessee planter. He died twelve years ago.

Betty Jones recalls when Evansville was a small town. She remembers when the street cars were mule drawn and people rode on them for pleasure. "When boats came in at Evansville, all the girls used to go down to the bank, wearing pretty ruffled dresses and every body would wave to the boat men and stay down at the river's edge until the boat was out of sight." Betty Jones remembers when the new Court House was started and how glad the men of the city were to erect the nice building. She recalls when the old frame buildings used for church services were razed and new structures were erected in which to worship God. She does not believe in evil spirits, ghosts nor charms as do many former slaves, but she remembers hearing her friends express superstitions concerning black cats. It was also a belief that to build a new kitchen onto your old home was always followed by the death of a member of the immediate family and if a bird flew into a window it had come to bring a call to the far away land and some member of the family would die.

Betty Jones was not scared when the recent flood came to within a block of her door. She had lived through a flood while living at Lawrence Station at Marion County, Indiana. "We was all marooned in our homes for two weeks and all the food we had was brought to our door by boats. White river was flooded then and our home was in the White River Flats." "What God wills must happen to us, and we do not save ourselves by trying to run away. Just as well stay and face it as to try to get away."

The old negro woman is cared for by her unmarried daughter since her husband's death. The old woman is lonely and was happy to recieve a caller. She is alone much of the time as her daughter is compelled to do house work to provide for her mother and herself. "Of course I'm a Christian," said the aged negress. "I'm a religious woman and hope to meet my friends in Heaven." "I would like to go back to Henderson, Kentucky once more, for I have not been there for more than twenty years. I'd live to walk the old plank walk again up to Mr. Alvis' home but I'm afraid I'll never get to go. It costs too much."

So desire remains with the aged and memories remain to comfort the feeble.

Federal Writers' Project
of the W.P.A.
District #6
Marion County
Anna Pritchett
1200 Kentucky Avenue

FOLKLORE
NATHAN JONES—EX-SLAVE
409 Blake Street

NATHAN JONES

Nathan Jones was born in Gibson County, Tennessee in 1858, the son of Caroline Powell, one of Parker Crimm's slaves.

Master Crimm was very abusive and cruel to his slaves. He would beat them for any little offense. He took pleasure in taking little children from their mothers and selling them, sending them as far away as possible.

Nathan's stepfather, Willis Jones, was a very strong man, a very good worker, and knew just enough to be resentful of his master's cruel treatment, decided to run away, living in the woods for days. His master sent out searchers for him, who always came in without him. The day of the sale, Willis made his appearance and was the first slave to be put on the block.

His new master, a Mr. Jones of Tipton, Tennessee, was very kind to him. He said it was a real pleasure to work for Mr. Jones as he had such a kind heart and respected his slaves.

Nathan remembers seeing slaves, both men and women, with their hands and feet staked to the ground, their faces down, giving them no chance to resist the overseers, whipped with cow hides until the blood gushed from their backs. "A very cruel way to treat human beings."

Nathan married very young, worked very hard, started buying a small orchard, but was "figgered" out of it, and lost all he had put into it. He then went to Missouri, stayed there until the death of his wife. He then came to Indiana, bringing his six children with him.

Forty-five years ago he married the second time; to that union were four children. He is very proud of his ten children and one stepchild.

His children have all been very helpful to him until times "got bad" with them, and could barely exist themselves.

Interviewer's Comment

Mr. and Mrs. Jones room with a family by the name of James; they have a comfortable, clean room and are content.

They are both members of the Free Will Baptist Church; get the old age pension, and "do very well."

Submitted December 15, 1937
Indianapolis, Indiana

Albert Strope, Field Worker
Federal Writers' Project
St. Joseph County—District #1
Mishawaka, Indiana

ADELINE ROSE LENNOX—EX-SLAVE
1400 South Sixth Street, Elkhart, Indiana

ADELINE ROSE LENNOX

Adeline Rose Lennox was born of slave parents at Middle—sometimes known as Paris—Tennessee, October 25, 1849. She lived with her parents in slave quarters on the plantation of a Mr. Rose for whom her parents worked. These quarters were log houses, a distance from the master's mansion.

At the age of seven years, Adeline was taken from her parents to work at the home of a son of Mr. Rose who had recently been married. She remembers well being taken away, for she said she cried, but her new mistress said she was going to have a new home so she had to go with her.

At the age of fourteen years she did the work of a man in the field, driving a team, plowing, harrowing and seeding. "We all thought a great deal of Mr. Rose," said Mrs. Lennox, "for he was good to us." She said that they were well fed, having plenty of corn, peas, beans, and pork to eat, more pork then than now.

As Adeline Rose, the subject of this sketch was married to Mr. Steward, after she was given her freedom at the close of the Civil War. At this time she was living with her parents who stayed with Mr. Rose for about five years after the war. To the Steward family was born one son, Johnny. Mr. Steward died early in life, and his widow married a second time, this time [HW: to] one George Lennox whose name she now bears.

Johnny married young and died young, leaving her alone in the world with the exception of her daughter-in-law. After her second husband's death, she remained near Middle, Tennessee, until 1924, when she removed to Elkhart to spend the remainder of her life living with her daughter-in-law, who had remarried and is now living at 1400 South Sixth Street, Elkhart, Indiana.

In the neighborhood she is known only as "Granny." While I was having this interview, a colored lady passed and this conversation followed:

"Good morning Granny, how are you this morning?"

"Only tolerable, thank you," replied Granny.

The health of Mrs. Lennox has been failing for the past three years but she gets around quite well for a lady who will be eight-eight years old the twenty-fifth day of this October. She gets an old age pension of about thirteen dollars per month.

A peculiar thing about Mrs. Lennox's life is that she says that she never knew that she was a slave until she was set free. Her mistress then told her that she was free and could go back to her father's home which she did rather reluctantly.

Mrs. Lennox smokes, enjoys corn bread and boiled

potatoes as food, but does not enjoy automobiles as "they are too bumpy and they gather too much air," she says. "I do not eat sweets," she remarks "my one am-bition in life is to live so that I may claim Heaven as my home when I die."

There is a newspaper picture in the office along with an article published by the Elkhart Truth. This is being sent to Indianapolis today.

Submitted by:
Estella R. Dodson
District #11
Monroe County
Bloomington, Ind.
October 4, 1937

INTERVIEW WITH THOMAS LEWIS, COLORED
North Summit Street, Bloomington, Ind.

THOMAS LEWIS

I was born in Spencer County, Kentucky, in 1857. I was born a slave. There was slavery all around on all the adjoining places. I was seven years old when I was set free. My father was killed in the Northern army. My mother, step-father and my mother's four living children came to Indiana when I was twelve years old. My grandfather was set free and given a little place of about sixteen acres. A gang of white men went to my grandmother's place and ordered the colored people out to work. The colored people had worked before for white men, on shares. When the wheat was all in and the corn laid by, the white farmers would tell the colored people to get out, and would give them nothing. The colored people did not want to work that way, and refused. This was the cause of the raids by white farmers. My mother recognized one of the men in the gang and reported him to the standing soldiers in Louisville. He was caught and made to tell who the others were until they had 360 men. All were fined and none allowed to leave until all the fines were paid. So the rich ones had to pay for the poor ones.

Many of them left because all were made responsible if such an event ever occurred again.

Our family left because we did not want to work that way. I was hired out to a family for $20 a year. I was sent for. My mother put herself under the protection of the police until we could get away. We came in a wagon from our home to Louisville. I was anxious to see Louisville, and thought it was very wonderful. I wanted to stay there, but we came on across the Ohio River on a ferry boat and stayed all night in New Albany. Next morning the wagon returned home and we came to Bloomington on the train. It took us from 9 o'clock until three in the evening to get here. There were big slabs of wood on the sides of the track to hold the rails together. Strips of iron were bolted to the rails on the inside to brace them apart. There were no wires at the joints of the rails to carry electricity, as we have now, for there was no electricity in those days.

I have lived in Bloomington ever since I came here. I met a family named Dorsett after I came here. They came from Jefferson County, Kentucky. Two of their daughters had been sold before the war. After the war, when the black people were free, the daughters heard some way that their people were in Bloomington. It was a happy time when they met their parents.

Once when I was a little boy, I was sitting on the fence while my mother plowed to get the field ready to put in wheat. The white man who owned her was plowing too. Some Yankee soldiers on horses came along. One rode up to the fence and when my mother came to the end of the furrow, he said to her, "Lady, could you tell me where Jim Downs' still house is?" My mother started to answer, but the man who owned her told her to move on. The soldiers told him to keep quiet, or they would make him sorry. After he went away, my mother told the soldiers where the house was. The reason her master did not want her to tell where the house was, was that some of his Rebel friends were hiding there. Spies had reported them to the Yankee soldiers. They went to the house and captured the Rebels.

Next soldiers came walking. I had no cap. One soldier asked me why I did not wear a cap. I said I had no cap. The soldier said, "You tell your mistress I said to buy you a cap or I'll come back and kill the whole family." They bought me a cap, the first one I ever had.

The soldiers passed for three days and a half. They were getting ready for a battle. The battle was close. We could hear the cannon. After it was over, a white man went to the battle field. He said that for a mile and a half one could walk on dead men and dead horses. My mother wanted to go and see it, but they wouldn't let her, for it was too awful.

I don't know what town we were near. The only town I know about had only about four or five houses and a mill. I think the name was Fairfield. That may not be the name, and the town may not be there any more. Once they sent my mother there in the forenoon. She saw a flash, and something hit a big barn. The timbers flew every way, and I suppose killed men and horses that were in the barn. There were Rebels hidden in the barn and in the houses, and a Yankee spy had found out where they were. They bombed the barn and surrounded the town. No one was able to leave. The Yankees came and captured the Rebels.

I had a cousin named Jerry. Just a little while before

the barn was struck a white man asked Jerry how he would like to be free. Jerry said that he would like it all right. The white men took him into the barn and were going to put him over a barrel and beat him half to death. Just as they were about ready to beat him, the bomb struck the barn and Jerry escaped. The man who owned us said for us to say that we were well enough off, and did not care to be free, just to avoid beatings. There was no such thing as being good to slaves. Many people were better than others, but a slave belonged to his master and there was no way to get out of it. A strong man was hard to make work. He would fight so that the white men trying to hold him would be breathless. Then there was nothing to do but kill him. If a slave resisted, and his master killed him, it was the same as self-defense today. If a cruel master whipped a slave to death, it put the fear into the other slaves. The brother of the man who owned my mother had many black people. He was too mean to live, but he made it. Once he was threshing wheat with a 'ground-hog' threshing machine, run by horse power. He called to a woman slave. She did not hear him because of the noise of the machine, and did not answer. He leaped off the machine to whip her. He caught his foot in some cogs and injured it so that it had to be taken off.

They tell me that today there is a place where there is a high fence. If someone gets near, he can hear the cries of the spirits of black people who were beaten to death. It is kept secret so that people won't find it out. Such places are always fenced to keep them secret. Once a man was out with a friend, hunting. The dog chased something back of a high fence. One man started to go in. The other said, "What are you going to do?" The other one said, "I want to see what the dog chased back in there." His friend told him, "You'd better stay out of there. That place is haunted by spirits of black people who were beaten to death."

Federal Writers' Project
of the W.P.A.
District #6
Marion County
Anna Pritchett
1200 Kentucky Avenue

FOLKLORE
MRS. SARAH H. LOCKE—DAUGHTER [of Wm. A. and Priscilla Taylor]

MRS. SARAH H. LOCKE

Mrs. Locke, the daughter of Wm. A. and Priscilla Taylor, was born in Woodford County, Kentucky in 1859. She went over her early days with great interest.

Jacob Keephart, her master, was very kind to his slaves, would never sell them to "nigger traders." His family was very large, so they bought and sold their slaves within the families and neighbors.

Mrs. Locke's father, brothers, and grandmother belonged to the same master in Henry County, Kentucky. Her mother and the two sisters belonged to another branch of the Keephart family, about seven miles away.

Her father came to see her mother on Wednesday and Saturday nights. They would have big dinners on these nights in their cabin.

Her father cradled all the grain for the neighborhood. He was a very high tempered man and would do no work when angry; therefore, every effort was made to keep him in a good humor when the work was heavy.

Her mother died when the children were very young. Sarah was given to the Keephart daughter as a wedding present and taken to her new home. She was always treated like the others in the family.

After the abolition of slavery, Mr Keephart gave Wm. a horse and rations to last for six months, so the children would not starve.

Charles and Lydia French, fellow workers with the Taylors, went to Cincinnatti and in 1867 sent for the Mrs. Locke and her sister, so they could go to school, as there were no schools in Kentucky then. The girls stayed one year with the French family; that is the longest time they ever went to school. After that, they would go to school for three months at different times. Mrs. Locke reads and writes very well.

The master worked right along with the slaves, shearing the sheep.

The women milk ten or twelve cows and knit a whole sock in one day. They also wove the material for their dresses; it was called "linsey."

She remembers one night the slaves were having a dance in one of the cabins, a band of Ku Kluxers came, took all firearms they could find, but no one was hurt, all wondered why, however, it did not take long for them to find out why. Another night when the Kluxers were riding, the slaves recognised the voice of their young master. That was the reason why the Keephart slaves were never molested.

Christmas was a jolly time for the Keephart slaves. They would have a whole week to celebrate, eating, dancing, and making merry.

"Free born niggers" were not allowed to associate with the slaves, as they were supposed to have no sense, and would contaminate the slaves.

Interviewer's Comment

Mrs. Locke is an intelligent old lady, has been a good dressmaker, and served for a great number of the "first families" of Indianapolis.

She has been married twice; her first husband died shortly after their marriage, and she was a widow for twenty-five years before she took her second "venture."

She gets the old age pension and is very happy.

Submitted December 17, 1937
Indianapolis, Indiana

Federal Writers' Project
of the W.P.A.
District #6
Marion County
Anna Pritchett
1200 Kentucky Avenue, Indianapolis, Indiana

FOLKLORE
ROBERT MCKINLEY—EX-SLAVE
1664 Columbia Avenue, Indianapolis, Indiana

ROBERT MCKINLEY

Robert McKinley was born in Stanley County, N.C., in 1849, a slave of Arnold Parker.

His master was a very cruel man, but was always kind to him, because he had given him (Bob) as a present to his favorite daughter, Jane Alice, and she would never permit anyone to mistreat Bob.

Miss Jane Alice was very fond of little Bob, and taught him to read and write.

His master owned a large farm, but Jane Alice would not let little Bob work on the farm. Instead, he helped his master in the blacksmith shop.

His master always prepared himself to whip his slaves by drinking a large glass of whiskey to give him strength to beat his slaves.

Robert remembers seeing his master beat his mother

until she would fall to the ground, and he was helpless to protect her. He would just have to stand and watch.

He has seen slaves tied to trees and beaten until the master could beat no longer; then he would salt and pepper their backs.

Once when the Confederate soldiers came to their farm, Robert told them where the liquor was kept and where the stock had been hidden. For this the soldiers gave him a handful of money, but it did him no good for his master took it away from him.

The McKinley family, of course, were Parkers and after the Civil war, they took the name of their father who was a slave of John McKinley.

A neighbor farmer, Jesse Hayden, was very kind to his slaves, gave them anything they wanted to eat, because he said they had worked hard, and made it possible for him to have all he had, and it was part theirs.

The Parker slaves were not allowed to associate with the Hayden slaves. They were known as the "rich niggers, who could eat meat without stealing it."

When the "nigger traders" came to the Parker farm, the old mistress would take meat skins and grease the mouths of the slave children to make it appear she had given them meat to eat.

Interviewer's Comment

Mr. McKinley is an "herb doctor" and lives very poorly in a dirty little house; he was very glad to tell of his early life.

He thinks people live too fast these days, and don't remember there is a stopping place.

Submitted January 10, 1938
Indianapolis, Indiana

Federal Writers' Project
of the W.P.A.
District #6
Marion County
Anna Pritchett
1200 Kentucky Avenue

FOLKLORE
RICHARD MILLER—AN OLD SOLDIER
1109 North West Street

RICHARD MILLER

Richard Miller was born January 12, 1843 in Danville, Kentucky. His mother was an English subject, born in Bombay, India and was brought into America by a group of people who did not want to be under the English government. They landed in Canada, came on to Detroit, stayed there a short time, then went to Danville, Kentucky. There she married a slave named Miller. They were the parents of five children.

After slavery was abolished, they bought a little farm a few miles from Danville, Kentucky.

The mother was very ambitious for her children, and sent them to the country school.

One day, when the children came home from school, their mother was gone; they knew not where.

It was learned, she was sending her children to school, and that was not wanted. She was taken to Texas, and nothing, was heard from her until 1871.

She wrote her brother she was comming to see them, and try to find her children, if any of them were left.

The boy, Richard, was in the army. He was so anxious to see his mother, to see what she would look like. The last time he saw her, she was washing clothes at the branch, and was wearing a blue cotton dress. All he could remember about her was her beautiful black hair, and the cotton dress. When he saw her, he didnot recognize her, but she told him of things he could remember that had happened, and that made him think she was his mother.

Richard was told who had taken the mother from the children, went to the man, shot and killed him; nothing was done to him for his deed.

He remembers a slave by the name of Brown, in Texas, who was chained hand and feet to a woodpile, oil thrown over him, and the wood, then fire set to the wood, and he was burned to death.

After the fire smoldered down, the white women and children took his ashes for souvenirs.

When slavery was abolished, a group of them started down to the far south, to buy farms, to try for themselves, got as far as Madison County, Kentucky and were told if they went any farther south, they would be made slaves again, not knowing if that was the truth or not, they stayed there, and worked on the Madison County farms for a very small wage. This separated families, and they never heard from each other ever again.

These separations are the cause of so many of the slave race not being able to trace families back for generations, as do the white families.

George Band was a very powerful slave, always ready to fight, never losing a fight, always able to defend himself until one night a band of Ku Kluxers came to his house, took his wife, hung her to a tree, hacked her to death with knives. Then went to the house, got George, took him to see what they had done to his wife. He asked them to let him go back to the house to get something to wrap his wife in, thinking he was sincere in his request, they allowed him to go. Instead of getting a wrapping for his wife, he got his Winchester rifle, shot and killed fourteen of the Kluxers. The county was never bothered with the Klan again. However, George left immediately for the North.

The first Monday of the month was sale day. The slaves were chained together and sent down in Miss., often separating mothers from children, husbands from wives, never to hear of each other again.

Interviewer's Comment

Mr. Miller lives with his family in a very comfortable home.

He has only one eye, wears a patch over the bad one.

He does not like to talk of his early life as he said it was such a "nightmare" to him; however he answered all questions very pleasantly.

Submitted December 9, 1937
Indianapolis, Indiana

William R. Mays
District 4
Johnson County

HENRY CLAY MOORMAN
BORN IN SLAVERY IN KENTUCKY
427 W. King St., Franklin, Ind.

HENRY CLAY MOORMAN

H enry Clay Moorman has resided in Franklin 34 years, he was born Oct. 1, 1854 in slavery on the Moorman plantation in Breckenridge County, Kentucky.

Mr. Moorman relates his own personal experiences as well as those handed down from his mother. He was a boy about 12 years old when freedom was declared. His father's name was Dorah Moorman who was a cooper by trade, and had a wife and seven children. They belonged to James Moorman, who owned about 20 slaves, he was kind to his slaves and never whipped any of them. These slaves loved their master and was as loyal to him as his own family.

Mr. Moorman says that when a boy he did small jobs around the plantation such as tobacco planting and going to the mill. One day he was placed upon a horse with a sack of grain containing about two bushels, after the sack of grain was balanced upon the back of the horse he was started to the mill which was a distance of about five miles, when about half the distance of the journey the sack of grain became unbalanced and fell from the horse being too small to lift the sack of grain he could only cry over the misfortune. There he was, powerless to do any thing about it. After about two hours there was a white man riding by and seeing the predicament he was in kindly lifted the sack up on the horse and after ascertaining his master's name bade him to continue to the mill. It was the custom at the mill that each await their turn, and do their own grinding. After the miller had taken his toll, he returned to his master and told of his experience. Thereafter precautions were taken so he would not again have the same experience.

The slave owners had so poisoned the minds of the slaves, they were in constant fear of the soldiers. One day when the slaves were alone at the plantation they sighted the Union soldiers approaching, they all went to the woods and hid in the bushes. The smaller children were covered with leaves. There they remained all night, as the soldiers (about 200 in number) camped all night in the horse lot. These soldiers were very orderly; however, they appropriated for their own use all the food they could find.

The slave owners would hide all their silverware and other articles of worth under the mattresses that were in the negro cabins for safe keeping.

There were three white children in the master's family. Wickliff, the oldest boy and Bob was the second child in age. The younger child, a girl, was named Sally and was about the same age as the subject of this article. Both children, being babies about the same age, the black mother served as a wet nurse for the white child, sometimes both the black child and the white child were upon the black mammies lap which frequently was the cause of battles between the two babies.

Some of the white mistresses acted as midwife for the black mothers.

There were two graveyards on the plantation, one for the white folks and one for the blacks. There is no knowledge of any deaths among the white folks during the time he lived on the plantation. One of this black boys' sisters married just before slavery was abolished. He remembers this wedding. In connection with the marriages of the slaves in slavery days, it is recalled that slaves seldom married among themselves on the same plantation but instead the unions were made by some negro boy from some other plantation courting a negro girl on a distant plantation. As was the custom in slavery days the black boy would have to get the consent of three people before he was allowed to enter upon wedlock; first, he would get the consent of the negro girls' mother, then he would get the consent of his own master as well as the black girl's master. This required time and diplomacy. When all had given their consent the marriage would take place usually on Saturday night, when a great time was had with slaves coming from other plantations with a generous supply of fried chicken, hams, cakes and pies a great feast and a good time generally with music and dancing. The new husband had to return to his own master after the wedding but it was understood by all that the new husband could visit his wife every Saturday night and stay until Monday morning. He would return every Monday to his master and work as usual indefinitely unless by chance one or the other of the two masters would buy the husband or wife, in such event they would live together as man and wife. Unless this purchase did occur it was the rule in slavery days that any children born to the slave wife would be the property of the girl's master.

When the required consent could not be had from all parties concerned it sometimes caused friction and instances have occured when attempts at elopement was made causing no end of trouble. This condition was very rare, as in most all cases of this kind the masters were quite willing for this marriage and would encourage the young couple. It is remembered that there were no illegitimate children born on the Moorman plantation.

The slaves would have their parties and dances. Slaves would gather from various plantations and these parties would sometimes last all night. It was customary for the slaves to get passes from their masters permitting them to attend, but sometimes passes were not given for reasons. In line with these parties it is remembered that there existed at that time what was known as the Paddle-Rollers, these so called Paddy-Rollers was made up of a bunch of white boys who would sneak up on these defenseless negroes unawares late in the night and demand that all show their passes. Those that could not show passes were whipped, both the negro boys and girls alike. The loyalty of these poor black boys was shown when they would volunteer to take an extra flogging to protect their girl friends. The Paddy-Rollers were a mean bunch of white boys who reviled in this shameful practice.

After slavery was abolished, this colored slave family remained on the same plantation for one year. They left the plantation via Cloverport by boat for Evansville, Ind., where they remained until the subject of this sketch removed to Franklin, Ind. in 1903 where he took pastorate with the African Methodist Episcopal Church where he served for 12 years. He is now a retired minister residing at 427 W. King St.

Federal Writers' Project
of the W.P.A.
District #6
Marion County
Anna Pritchett
1200 Kentucky Avenue

FOLKLORE
MRS. AMERICA MORGAN—EX-SLAVE
816 Camp Street

MRS. AMERICA MORGAN

America Morgan was born in a log house, daubed with dirt, in Ballard County, Kentucky, in 1852, the daughter of Manda and Jordon Rudd. She remembers very clearly the happenings of her early life.

Her mother, Manda Rudd, was owned by Clark Rudd, and the "devil has sure got him."

Her father was owned by Mr. Willingham, who was very kind to his slaves. Jordon became a Rudd, because he was married to Manda on the Rudd plantation.

There were six children in the family, and all went well until the death of the mother; Clark Rudd whipped her to death when America was five years old.

Six little children were left motherless to face a "frowning world."

America was given to her master's daughter, Miss Meda, to wait on her, as her personal property. She lived with her for one year, then was sold for $600.00 to Mr. and Mrs. Utterback stayed with them until the end of the Civil war.

The new mistress was not so kind. Miss Meda, who knew her reputation, told her if she abused America, she would come for her, and she would loose the $600.00 she had paid for her. Therefore, America was treated very kindly.

Aunt Catherine, who looked after all the children on the plantation, was very unruly, no one could whip her. Once America was sent for two men to come and tie Aunt Catherine. She fought so hard, it was as much as the men could do to tie her. They tied her hands, then hung her to the joist and lashed her with a cow hide. It "was awful to hear her screams."

In 1865 her father came and took her into Paduca, Kentucky, "a land of freedom."

When thirteen years old, America did not know A from B, then "glory to God," a Mr. Greeleaf, a white man, from the north, came down to Kentucky and opened a school for Negro children. That was America's first chance to learn. He was very kind and very sympathetic. She went to school for a very short while.

Her father was very poor, had nothing at all to give his children.

America's mistress would not give her any of her clothes. "All she had in this world, was what she had on her back." Then she was "hired out" for $1.00 a week.

The white people for whom she worked were very

kind to her and would try to teach her when her work was done. She was given an old fashioned spelling book and a first reader. She was then "taught much and began to know life."

She was sent regularly to church and Sunday school. That was when she began to "wake up" to her duty as a free girl.

The Rev. D.W. Dupee was her Sunday school teacher, from him she learned much she had never known before.

At seventeen years of age, she married and "faced a frowning world right." She had a good husband and ten children, three of whom are living today, one son and two daughters.

She remembers one slave, who had been given five hundred lashes on his back, thrown in his cabin to die. He laid on the floor all night, at dawn he came to himself, and there were blood hounds licking his back.

When the overseers lashed a slave to death, they would turn the bloodhounds out to smell the blood, so they would know "nigger blood," that would help trace runaway slaves.

Aunt Jane Stringer was given five hundred lashes and thrown in her cabin. The next morning when the overseer came, he kicked her and told her to get up, and wanted to know if she was going to sleep there all day. When she did not answer him, he rolled her over and the poor woman was dead, leaving several motherless children.

When the slaves were preparing to run away, they

would put hot pepper on their feet; this would cause the hounds to be thrown off their trail.

Aunt Margaret ran off, but the hounds traced her to a tree; she stayed up in the tree for two days and would not come down until they promised not to whip her any more, and they kept their promise.

Old mistress' mother was sick a long time, and little America had to keep the flies off of her by waving a paper fly brush over her bed. She was so mean, America was afraid to go too near the bed for fear she might try to grab her and shake her. After she died, she haunted America. Anytime she would go into the room, she could hear her knocking on the wall with her cane. Some nights they would hear her walking up and down the stairs for long periods at a time.

Aunt Catherine ran off, because "ole missie" haunted her so bad.

The old master came back after his death and would ride his favorite horse, old Pomp, all night long, once every week. When the boy would go in to feed the horses, old Pomp would have his ears hanging down, and he would be "just worn out," after his night ride.

Interviewer's Comment

America believes firmly in haunts, and said she had lived in several haunted houses since coming up north.

Mrs. Morgan lives with her baby boy and his wife. She is rather inteligent, reads and writes, and tries to do all she can to help those who are less fortunate than she.

Submitted December 27, 1937
Indianapolis, Indiana

Iris Cook
District 4
Floyd County

STORY OF GEORGE MORRISON
25 East 5th St., New Albany, Ind.

GEORGE MORRISON

Observation of the writer

(This old negro, known as "Uncle George" by the neighbors, is very particular about propriety. He allows no woman in his house unless accompanied by a man. He says "It jest a'nt the proper thing to do", but he came to a neighbors for a little talk.)

"I was bawn in Union County, Kentucky, near Morganfield. My master was Mr. Ray, he made me call him Mr. Ray, wouldent let me call him Master. He said I was his little free negro."

When asked if there were many slaves on Mr. Ray's farm, he said, "Yes'm, they was seven cabin of us. I was the oldes' child in our family. Mr. Ray said "He didn't want me in the tobacco", so I stayed at the house and waited on the women folk and went after the cows when I was big enough. I carried my stick over my shoulder for I wus afraid of snakes."

"Mr. Ray was always very good to me, he liked to play with me, cause I was so full of tricks an' so mischuvus. He give me a pair of boots with brass toes. I shined them up ever day, til you could see your face in 'em."

"There wuz two ladies at the house, the Missus and her daughter, who was old enough to keep company when I was a little boy. They used to have me to drive 'em to church. I'd drive the horses. They'd say, 'George, you come in here to church.' But I always slipped off with the other boys who was standing around outside waitin' for they folks, and played marbles."

"Yes, ma'am, the War sho did affect my fambly. My father, he fought for the north. He got shot in his side, but it finally got all right. He saved his money and came north after the war and got a good job. But, I saw them fellows from the south take my Uncle. They put his clothes on him right in the yard and took him with them to fight. And even the white folks, they all cried. But he came back, he wasnt hurt but he wasent happy in his mind like my pappy was."

"Yes ma'am, I would rather live in the North. The South's all right but someways I just don't feel down there like I does up here."

"No ma'am, I was never married. I don't believe in getting married unless you got plenty of money. So many married folks dont do nuthin but fuss and fight. Even my father and mother always spatted and I never liked that and so I says to myself what do I want to get married for. I'm happier just living by myself."

"Yes Ma'am. I remember when people used to take wagon loads of corn to the market in Louisville, and they would bring back home lots of groceries and things.

A colored man told me he had come north to the market in Louisville with his master, and was working hard unloading the corn when a white man walks up to him, shows him some money and asks him if he wanted to be free? He said he stopped right then and went with the man, who hid him in his wagon under the provisions and they crossed the Ohio River right on the ferry. That's the way lots of 'em got across here."

"Did I ever hear of any ghosts. Yes ma'am I have. I hear noises and I seed something once that I never could figger out. I was goin't thru the woods one day, and come up sudden in a clear patch of ground. There sat a little boy on a stump, all by his-self, there in the woods. I asks him who he wuz & wuz he lost, and he never answered me. Jest sat there, lookin at me. All of a sudden he ups and runs, and I took out after him. He run behind a big tree, and when I got up to where I last seed him, he wuz gone. And there sits a great big brown man twice as big as me, on another stump. He never seys a word, jest looks at me. And then I got away from there, yes ma'am I really did."

"A man I knew saw a ghost once and he hit at it. He always said he wasn't afraid of no ghost, but that ghost hit him, and hit him so hard it knocked his face to one side and the last time I saw him it was still that way. No ma'am, I don't really believe in ghosts, but you know how it is, I lives by myself and I don't like to talk about them for you never can tell what they might do.

"Lady you ought to hear me rattle bones, when I was young. I caint do it much now for my wrists are too stiff. When they played Turkey in the Straw how we all used to dance and cut up. We'ed cut the pigeon wing, and buck the wind [HW: wing?], and all. But I got rewmaytism in my feet now and ant much good any more, but I sure has done lots of things and had lots of fun in my time."

Federal Writers' Project
of the W.P.A.
District #6
Marion County
Anna Pritchett
1200 Kentucky Avenue, Indianapolis, Indiana

FOLKLORE
JOSEPH MOSLEY, EX-SLAVE
2637 Boulevard Place

[TR: Also reported as Moseley in text of interview.]

JOSEPH MOSLEY

Joseph Mosley, one of twelve children, was born March 15, 1853, fourteen miles from Hopkinsville, Kentucky.

His master, Tim Mosley, was a slave trader. He was supposed to have bought and sold 10,000 slaves. He would go from one state to another buying slaves, bringing in as many as 75 or 80 slaves at one time.

The slaves would be handcuffed to a chain, each chain would link 16 slaves. The slaves would walk from Virginia to Kentucky, and some from Mississippi to Virginia.

In front of the chained slaves would be an overseer on horseback with a gun and dogs. In back of the chained slaves would be another overseer on horseback with a gun and dogs. They would see that no slave escaped.

Joseph's father was the shoemaker for all the farm

hands and all adult workers. He would start in September making shoes for the year. First the shoes for the folks in the house, then the workers.

No slave child ever wore shoes, summer or winter.

The father, mother, and all the children were slaves in the same family, but not in the same house. Some with the daughters, some with the sons, and so on. No one brother or sister would be allowed to visit with the others.

After the death of Tim Moseley, little Joseph was given to a daughter. He was seven years old; he had to pick up chips, tend the cows, and do small jobs around the house; he wore no clothing except a shirt.

Little Joseph did not see his mother after he was taken to the home of the daughter until he was set free at the age of 13.

The master was very unkind to the slaves; they sometimes would have nothing to eat, and would eat from the garbage.

On Christmas morning Joseph was told he could go see his mother; he did not know he was free, and couldn't understand why he was given the first suit of clothes he had ever owned, and a pair of shoes. He dressed in his new finery and was started out on his six mile journey to his mother.

He was so proud of his new shoes; after he had gotten out of sight, he stopped and took his shoes off as he did not want them dirty before his mother had seen them, and walked the rest of the way in his bare feet.

After their freedom, the family came to Indiana.

The mother died here, in Indianapolis, at the age of 105.

Interviewer's Comment

Mr. Moseley, who has been in Indianapolis for 35 years, has been paralyzed for the last four years. He and a daughter room with a Mrs. Turner.

He has a very nice clean room; a very pleasant old man was very glad to talk of his past life.

He gets a pension of $18.00 a month, and said it was not easy to get along on that little amount, and wondered if the government was ever going to increase his pension.

Submitted December 1, 1937
Indianapolis, Indiana

United States. Work Projects Administration

Ex-Slave Stories
District #5
Vanderburgh County
Lauana Creel

MEMORIES OF SLAVERY AND THE LIFE STORY OF
AMY ELIZABETH PATTERSON

AMY ELIZABETH PATTERSON

The slave mart, separation from a dearly beloved mother and little sisters are among the earliest memories recalled by Amy Elizabeth Patterson, a resident of Evansville, Indiana.

Amy Elizabeth, now known as "Grandmother Patterson" resides with her daughter Lula B. Morton at 512 Linwood Avenue near Cherry Street. Her birth occurred July 12, 1850 at Cadiz, Trigg County, Kentucky. Her mother was Louisa Street, slave of John Street, a merchant of Cadez. [TR: likely Cadiz]

"John Street was never unkind to his slaves" is the testimony of Grandmother Patterson, as she recalls and relates stories of the long ago. "Our sorrow began when slave traders, came to Cadiz and bought such slaves as he took a fancy to and separated us from our families!"

John Street ran a sort of agency where he collected slaves and yearly sold them to dealers in human flesh. Those he did not sell he hired out to other families. Some were hired or indentured to farmers, some to stock raisers, some to merchants and some to captains of boats and the hire of all these slaves went into the coffers of John Street, yearly increasing his wealth.

Louisa Street, mother of Amy Elizabeth Patterson, was house maid at the Street home and her first born daughter was fair with gold brown hair and amber eyes. Mr. and Mrs. Street always promised Louisa they would never sell her as they did not want to part with the child, so Louisa was given a small cabin near the master's house. The mistress had a child near the age of the little mulatto and Louisa was wet nurse for both children as well as maid to Mrs. Street. Two years after the birth of Amy Elizabeth, Louisa became mother of twin daughters, Fannie and Martha Street, then John Street decided to sell all his slaves as he contemplated moving into another territory.

The slaves were auctioned to the highest bidder and Louisa and the twins were bought by a man living near Cadiz but Mr. Street refused to sell Amy Elizabeth. She showed promise of growing into an excellent house-maid and seamstress and was already a splendid playmate and nurse to the little Street boy and girl. So Louisa lost her child but such grief was shown by both mother and child that the mother was unable to perform her tasks and the child cried continually. Then Mr. Street consented to sell the little girl to the mother's new master.

Louisa Street became mother of seventeen children. Three were almost white. Amy Elizabeth was the daughter of John Street and half sister of his children by his lawful wife. Mrs. Street knew the facts and respected Louisa and her child and, says grandmother Patterson, "That was the greatest crime ever visited on the United States. It was worse than the cruelty of the overseers, worse than hunger, for many slaves were well fed and well cared for;

but when a father can sell his own child, humiliate his own daughter by auctioning her on the slave block, what good could be expected where such practices were allowed?"

Grandmother Patterson remembers superstitions of slavery days and how many slaves were afraid of ghosts and evil spirits but she never believed in supernatural appearances until three years ago when she received a message, through a medium, from the spirit land; now she is a firm believer, not in ghosts and evil visitations, but in true communication with the departed ones who still love and long to protect those who remain on earth.

Several years ago a young grandson of the old woman was drowned. The little boy was Stokes Morton, a very popular child rating high averages in school studies and beloved by his teachers and friends. The mother, Lulu B. Morton and the grandmother both gave up to grief, in fact they both have declined in health and were unable to carry on their regular duties.

Grandmother Patterson began suffering from a dental ailment and was compelled to visit a dental surgeon. The dental surgeon suggested that she visit a medium and seek some comforting message from the child.

She at once visited a medium and received a message. "Stokes answered me. In fact he was waiting to communicate with us. He said 'Grandmother! you and mother must stop staying at the cemetary and grieving for me. Send the flowers to your sick friends and put in more time with the other children. I am happy here, I am in a beautiful field, The sky is blue and the field is full of beautiful white lambs that play with me.'"

The message comforted the aged woman. She began occupying her time with other members of the family and again began to visit with her neighbors.

She felt a call two years later and again consulted the medium. That time she received a message from the child, his father and a little girl that had died in infancy. Grandmother Patterson said she would not recall the ones who had gone on to the land of promise. She is a christian and a believer in the Word of God.

Grandmother Patterson, in spite of her 87 years of life (fifteen of which were passed in slavery) is useful in her daughter's home. Her children and grand children are fond of her as indeed they well may be. She is a refined woman, gracious to every person she encounters. She is hoping for better opportunities for her race. She admonishes the younger relatives to live in the fear and love of the Lord that no evil days overtake them.

"Yes, slavery was a curse to this nation" she declares, "A curse which still shows itself in hundreds of homes where mulatto faces are evidence of a heinous sin and proof that there has been a time when American fathers sold their children at the slave marts of America." She is glad the curse has been erased even if by the bloodshed of heroes.

G. Monroe
Dist. 4
Jefferson County

SLAVE STORY
MRS. PRESTON'S STORY

MRS. PRESTON'S STORY

Mrs. Preston is an old lady, 83 years old, very charming and hospitable She lives on North Elm Street, Madison, Indiana. Her first recollections of slavery were of sleeping on the foot of her mistress' bed, where she could get up during the night to "feed" the fire with chips she had gathered before dark or to get a drink or anything else her mistress might want in the night.

Her 'Marse Brown', resided in Frankfort having taken his best horses and hogs, and leaving his family in the care of an overseer on a farm. He was afraid the Union soldiers would kill him, but thought his wife would be safe. This opinion proved to be true. The overseer called the slaves to work at four o'clock, and they worked until six in the evening.

When Mrs. Preston was a little older part of her work was to drive about a dozen cows to and from the stable. Many a time she warmed her bare feet in the cattle bedding. She said they did not always go barefooted but their shoes were old or their feet wrapped in rags.

Her next promotion was to work in the fields haul-
ing shocks of corn on a balky mule which was subject
to bucking and throwing its rider over its head. She was
aided by a little boy on another mule. There were men to
tie the shocks and place them on the mule.

She remembered seeing Union and Confederate soldiers shooting across a river near her home. Her uncle
fought two years, and returned safely at the end of the
war.

She did not feel that her Master and Mistress had
mistreated their slaves. At the close of the war, her father
was given a house, land, team and enough to start farming for himself.

Several years later the Ku Klux Klan gave them a ten
days notice to leave, one of the masked band interceded
for them by pointing out that they were quiet and pea-
cable, and a man with a crop and ten children couldn't
possibly leave on so short a notice so the time was ex-
tended another ten days, when they took what the Klan
paid them and came north. They remained in the north
until they had to buy their groceries "a little piece of this
and a little piece of that, like they do now", when her
father returned to Kentucky. Mrs. Preston remained in
Indiana. Her father was burned out, the family escaping
to the woods in their night clothes, later befriended by a
white neighbor. Now they appealed to their former owner who built them a new house, provided necessities and
guards for a few weeks until they were safe from the Ku
Klux Klan.

Mrs. Preston said she was the mother of ten children,
but now lives alone since the death of her husband three

years ago. Her white neighbors say her house is so clean, one could almost eat off the floor.

Federal Writers' Project
of the W.P.A.
District #6
Marion County
Harry Jackson

WILLIAM M. QUINN (EX-SLAVE)
431 Bright Street, Indianapolis, Ind.

WILLIAM M. QUINN

William M. Quinn, 431 Bright street, was a slave up to ten years of age—"when the soldiers come back home, and the war was over, and we wasn't slaves anymore". Mr. Quinn was born in Hardin County, Kentucky, on a farm belonging to Steve Stone. He and a brother and his mother were slaves of "Old Master Stone", but his father was owned by another man, Mr. Quinn, who had an adjoining farm. When they were all freed, they took the surname of Quinn.

Mr. Quinn said that they were what was called "gift slaves". They were never to be sold from the Stone farm and were given to Stone's daughter as a gift with that understanding. He said that his "Old master paid him and his brother ten cents a day for cutting down corn and shucking it."

It was very unusual for a slave to receive any money whatsoever for working. He said that his master had a son about his age, and the son and he and his brother worked around the farm together, and "Master Stone" gave all three of them ten cents a day when they worked.

Sometimes they wouldn't, they would play instead. And whenever "Master Stone" would catch them playing when they ought to have been at work, he would whip them—"and that meant his own boy would get a licking too."

"Old Master Stone was a good man to all us colored folks, we loved him. He wasn't one of those mean devils that was always beating up his slaves like some of the rest of them." He had a colored overseer and one day this overseer ran off and hid for two days "cause he whipped one of old Mas' Stone's slaves and he heard that Mas' Stone was mad and he didn't like it."

"We didn't know that we were slaves, hardly. Well, my brother and I didn't know anyhow 'cause we were too young to know, but we knew that we had been when we got older."

"After emancipation we stayed at the Stone family for some time, 'cause they were good to us and we had no place to go." Mr. Quinn meant by emancipation that his master freed his slaves, and, as he said, "emancipated them a year before Lincoln did."

Mr. Quinn said that his father was not freed when his mother and he and his brother were freed, because his father's master "didn't think the North would win the war." Stone's slaves fared well and ate good food and "his own children didn't treat us like we were slaves." He said some of the slaves on surrounding plantations and farms had it "awful hard and bad." Some times slaves would run away during the night, and he said that "we would give them something to eat." He said his mother did the cooking for the Stone family and that she was good to runaway slaves.

Submitted September 9, 1937
Indianapolis, Indiana

United States. Work Projects Administration

Federal Writers' Project
of the W.P.A.
District #6
Marion County
Harry Jackson

EX SLAVE STORY
MRS. CANDUS RICHARDSON
[HW: Personal Interview]

MRS. CANDUS RICHARDSON

Mrs. Candus Richardson, of 2710 Boulevard Place, was 18 years of age when the Civil War was over. She was borned a slave on Jim Scott's plantation on the "Homer Chitter river" in Franklin county, Mississippi. Scott was the heir of "Old Jake Scott". "Old Jim Scott" had about fifty slaves, who raised crops, cotton, tobacco, and hogs. Candus cooked for Scott and his wife, Miss Elizabeth. They were both cruel, according to Mrs. Richardson. She said that at one time her Master struck her over the head with the butt end of a cowhide, that made a hole in her head, the scar of which she still carries. He struck her down because he caught her giving a hungry slave something to eat at the back door of the "big house". The "big house" was Scott's house.

Scott beat her husband a lot of times because he caught him praying. But "beatings didn't stop my husband from praying. He just kept on praying. He'd steal off to the woods and pray, but he prayed so loud that anybody close around could hear, 'cause he had such a loud voice. I prayed too, but I always prayed to myself." One time, Jim Scott beat her husband so unmerciful for praying that his shirt was as red from blood stain "as if you'd paint it with, a brush". Her husband was very religious, and she claimed that it was his prayers and "a whole lot of other slaves' that cause you young folks to be free today".

They didn't have any Bible on the Scott plantation she said, for it meant a beating or "a killing if you'd be caught with one". But there were a lot of good slaves and they knew how to pray and some of the white folks loved to hear than pray too, "'cause there was no put-on about it. That's why we folks know how to sing and pray, 'cause we have gone through so much, but the Lord is with us, the Lord's with us, he is".

Mrs. Richardson said that the slaves, that worked in the Master's house, ate the same food that the master and his family ate, but those out on the plantation didn't fare so well; they ate fat meats and parts of the hog that the folks at the "big house" didn't eat. All the slaves had to call Scott and his wife "Master and Miss Elizabeth", or they would get punished if they didn't.

Whenever the slaves would leave the plantation, they ware supposed to have a permit from Scott, and if they were caught out by the "padyrollers", they would whip them if they did not have a note from their master. When the slaves went to church, they went to a Baptist church that the Scotts belonged to and sat in the rear of the church. The sermon was never preached to the slaves. "They never preached the Lord to us," Mrs. Richardson said, "They would just tell us to not steal, don't steal from your master". A week's ration of food was given each slave, but if he ate it up before the week, he had to eat salt pork until the next rations. He couldn't eat much of it, because it was too salty to eat any quanity of it. "We had to make our own clothes out of a cloth like you use, called canvass". "We walked to church with our shoes on our arms to keep from wearing them out".

They walked six miles to reach the church, and had to wade across a stream of water. The women were carried across on the men's backs. They did all of this to hear the minister tell them "don't steal from your Master".

They didn't have an overseer to whip the slaves on the Scott plantation, Scott did the whipping himself. Mrs. Richardson said he knocked her down once just before she gave birth to a daughter, all because she didn't pick cotton as fast as he thought she should have.

Her husband went to the war to be "what you call a valet for Master Jim's son, Sam". After the war, he "came to me and my daughter". "Then in July, we could tell by the crops and other things grown, old Master Jim told us everyone we was free, and that was almost a year after the other slaves on the other plantations around were freed". She said Scott, in freeing (?) then said that "he didn't have to give us any thing to eat and that he didn't have to give us a place to stay, but we could stay and work for him and he would pay us. But we left that night and walked for miles through the rain to my husban's broth- er and then told them that they all were free. Then we all came up to Kentucky in a wagon and lived there. Then I came up North when my husband died".

Mrs. Richardson says that she is "so happy to know that I have lived to see the day when you young people can serve God without slipping around to serve him like we old folks had to do". "You see that pencil that you have In your hand there, why, that would cost me my life 'if old Mas' Jim would see me with a pencil in my hand. But I lived to see both him and Miss Elizabeth die a hard death. They both hated to die, although they belonged to church. Thank God for his mercy! Thank God!" "My mother prayed for me and I am praying for you young folks".

Mrs. Richardson, despite her 90 years of age, can walk a distance of a mile and a half to her church.

Submitted August 31, 1937
Indianapolis, Indiana

Federal Writers' Project
of the W.P.A.
District #6
Marion County
Anna Pritchett
1200 Kentucky Avenue

FOLKLORE
JOE ROBINSON—EX-SLAVE
1132 Cornell Avenue

JOE ROBINSON

Joe Robinson was born in Mason County, Kentucky in 1854.

His master, Gus Hargill, was very kind to him and all his slaves. He owned a large farm and raised every kind of vegetation. He always gave his slaves plenty to eat. They never had to steal food. He said his slaves had worked hard to permit him to have plenty, therefore they should have their share.

Joe, his mother, a brother, and a sister were all on the same plantation. They were never sold, lived with the same master until they were set free.

Joe's father was owned by Rube Black, who was very cruel to his slaves, beat them severely for the least offense. One day he tried to beat Joe's father, who was a large strong man; he resisted his master and tried to kill him. After that he never tried to whip him again. However, at the first opportunity, Rube sold him.

The Robinson family learned the father had been sold to someone down in Louisiana. They never heard from, or of him, again.

Interviewer's Comment

Mr. Robinson lives with his wife; he receives a pension, which he said was barely enough for them to live on, and hoped it would be increased.

He attends one of the W.P.A. classes, trying to learn to read and write.

They have two children who live in Chicago.

Submitted January 24, 1938
Indianapolis, Indiana

Federal Writers' Project
of the W.P.A.
District #6
Marion County
Anna Pritchett
1200 Kentucky Avenue, Indianapolis, Indiana

FOLKLORE
MRS. ROSALINE ROGERS—EX-SLAVE—110 YEARS OLD
910 North Capitol Avenue, Indianapolis, Indiana

MRS. ROSALINE ROGERS

Mrs. Rogers was born in South Carolina, in 1827, a slave of Dr. Rice Rogers, "Mas. Rogers," we called him, was the youngest son of a family of eleven children. He was so very mean.

Mrs. Rogers was sold and taken to Tennessee at the age of eleven for $900.00 to a man by the name of Carter. Soon after her arrival at the Carter plantation, she was resold to a man by the name of Belby Moore with whom she lived until the beginning of the Civil war.

Men and women were herded into a single cabin, no matter how many there were. She remembers a time when there were twenty slaves in a small cabin. There were holes between the logs of the cabin, large enough for dogs and cats to crawl through. The only means of heat, being a wood fireplace, which, of course, was used for cooking their food.

The slaves' food was corn cakes, side pork, and beans; seldom any sweets except molasses.

The slaves were given a pair of shoes at Christmas time and if they were worn out before summer, they were forced to go barefoot.

Her second master would not buy shoes for his slaves. When they had to plow, their feet would crack and bleed from walking on the hard clods, and if one complained, they would be whipped; therefore, very few complaints were made.

The slaves were allowed to go to their master's church, and allowed to sit in the seven back benches; should those benches be filled, they were not allowed to sit in any other benches.

The wealthy slave owner never allowed his slaves to pay any attention to the poor "white folks," as he knew they had been free all their lives and should be slave owners themselves. The poor whites were hired by those who didnot believe in slavery, or could not afford slaves.

At the beginning of the Civil war, I had a family of fourteen children. At the close of the war, I was given my choice of staying on the same plantation, working on shares, or taking my family away, letting them out for their food and clothes. I decided to stay on that way; I could have my children with me. They were not allowed to go to school, they were taught only to work.

Slave mothers were allowed to stay in bed only two or three days after childbirth; then were forced to go into the fields to work, as if nothing had happened.

The saddest moment of my life was when I was sold away from my family. I often wonder what happened to them, I haven't seen or heard from them since. I only hope God was as good to them as He has been to me.

"I am 110 years old; my birth is recorded in the slave book. I have good health, fairly good eyesight, and a good memory, all of which I say is because of my love for God."

Interviewer's Comment

Mrs. Rogers is certainly a very old woman, very pleasant, and seems very fond of her granddaughters, with whom she lives.

Submitted December 29, 1937
Indianapolis, Indiana

Federal writers' Project
of the W.P.A.
District #6
Marion County
Anna Pritchett
1200 Kentucky Avenue

FOLKLORE
MRS. PARTHENA ROLLINS
848 Camp Street (Rear)

MRS. PARTHENA ROLLINS

Mrs. Parthena Rollins was born in Scott County, Kentucky, in 1853, a slave of Ed Duvalle, who was always very kind to all of his slaves, never whipping any of the adults, but often whipped the children to correct them, never beating them. They all had to work, but never overwork, and always had plenty to eat.

She remembers so many slaves, who were not as fortunate as they were.

Once when the "nigger traders" came through, there was a girl, the mother of a young baby; the traders wanted the girl, but would not buy her because she had the child. Her owner took her away, took the baby from her, and beat it to death right before the mother's eyes, then brought the girl back to the sale without the baby, and she was bought immediately.

Her new master was so pleased to get such a strong girl who could work so well and so fast.

The thoughts of the cruel way of putting her baby to death preyed on her mind to such an extent, she developed epilepsy. This angered her new master, and he sent her back to her old master, and forced him to refund the money he had paid for her.

Another slave had displeased his master for some reason, he was taken to the barn and killed, and was buried right in the barn. No one knew of this until they were set free, as the slaves who knew about it were afraid to tell for fear of the same fate befalling on them.

Parthena also remembers slaves being beaten until their backs were blistered. The overseers would then open the blisters and sprinkle salt and pepper in the open blisters, so their backs would smart and hurt all the more.

Many times, slaves would be beaten to death, thrown into sink holes, and left for the buzzards to swarm and feast on their bodies.

So many of the slaves she knew were half fed and half clothed, and treated so cruelly, that it "would make your hair stand on ends."

Interviewer's Comment

Mrs. Rollins is in poor health all broken up with "rheumatiz."

She lives with a daughter and grandson, and said she could hardly talk of the happenings of the early days, because of the awful things her folks had to go through

Submitted December 21, 1937
Anatolia, Indiana

Ex-Slave Stories
District #5
Vanderburgh County
Lauana Creel

TOLD BY JOHN RUDD, AN EX-SLAVE

JOHN RUDD

"Yes, I was a slave," said John Rudd, "And I'll say this to the whole world, Slavery was the worst curse ever visited on the people of the United States."

John Rudd is a negro, dark and swarthy as to complexion but his nose is straight and aqualine, for his mother-was half Indian.

The memory of his mother, Liza Rudd, is sacred to John Rudd today and her many disadvantages are still a source of grief to the old man of 83 years. John Rudd was born on Christmas day 1854 in the home of Benjamin Simms, at Springfield, Kentucky. The mother of the young child was house maid for mistress Simms and Uncle John remembers that mother and child received only the kindliest consideration from all members of the Simms family.

While John was yet a small boy Benjamin Simms died and the Simms slaves were auctioned to the highest bidders. "If'n you wants to know what unhappiness means," said Uncle John Rudd, "Jess'n you stand on the

Slave Block and hear the Auctioneer's voice selling you away from the folks you love." Uncle John explained how mothers and fathers were often separated from their dearly loved children, at the auction block, but John and his younger brother Thomas were fortunate and were bought by the same master along with Liza Rudd, their mother. An elder brother, Henry, was separated from his mother and brothers and became the property of George Snyder and was thereafter known as Henry Snyder.

When Liza Rudd and her two little sons left the slave block they were the property of Henry Moore who lived a few miles away from Springfield. Uncle John declares that unhappiness met them at the threshold of the Moore's estate.

Liza was given the position of cook, housemaid and plough-hand while her little boys were made to hoe, carry wood and care for the small children of the Moore family.

John had only been at the Moore home a few months when he witnessed several slaves being badly beaten. Henry Moore kept a white overseer and several white men were employed to whip slaves. A large barrel stood near the slave quarters and the little boy discovered that the barrel was a whipping post. The slaves would be strapped across the side of the barrel and two strong men would wield the "cat of nine tails" until blood flowed from gashed flesh, and the cries and prayers of the unfortunate culprits availed them nothing until the strength of the floggers became exhausted.

One day, when several Negroes had just recovered from an unusual amount of chastisement, the little

Negro, John Rudd, was playing in the front yard of the Moore's house when he heard a soft voice calling him. He knew the voice belonged to Shell Moore, one of his best friends at the Moore estate. Shell had been among those severely beaten and little John had been grieving over his misfortunes. "Shell had been in the habbit of whittling out whistles for me and pettin' of me," said the now aged negro. "I went to see what he wanted wif me and he said 'Goodby Johnnie, you'll never see Shellie alive after today.'" Shell made his way toward the cornfield but the little Negro boy, watching him go, did not realize what situation confronted him. That night the master announced that Shell had run away again and the slaves were started searching fields and woods but Shell's body was found three days later by Rhoder McQuirk, dangling from a rafter of Moore's corn crib where the unhappy Negro had hanged himself with a leather halter.

Shell was a splendid worker and was well worth a thousand dollars. If he had been fairly treated he would have been happy and glad to repay kindness by toil. "Mars Henry would have been better to all of us, only Mistress Jane was always rilin' him up," declared John Rudd as he sat in his rocking chair under a shade tree.

"Jane Moore, was the daughter of Old Thomas Rakin, one of the meanest men, where slaves were concerned, and she had learnt the slave drivin' business from her daddy."

Uncle John related a story concerning his mother as follows: "Mama had been workin' in the cornfield all day 'till time to cook supper. She was jes' standin' in the smoke house that was built back of the big kitchen when Mistress walks in. She had a long whip hid under her apron and began whippin Mama across the shoulders, 'thout tellin' her why. Mama wheeled around from whar she was slicin' ham and started runnin' after old Missus Jane. Ole Missus run so fas' Mama couldn't catch up wif her so she throwed the butcher knife and stuck it in the wall up to the hilt." "I was scared. I was fraid when Marse Henry come in I believed he would have Mama whipped to death."

"Whar Jane?" said Mars Henry. "She up stairs with the door locked," said Mama. Then she tole old Mars Henry the truth about how mistress Jane whip her and show him the marks of the whip. She showed him the butcher knife stickin' in the wall. "Get yer clothes to-gether," said Marse Henry.

John then had to be parted from his mother. Henry Rudd [TR: 'Moore' written above in brackets.] believed that the Negroes were going to be set free. War had been declared and his desire was to send Liza far into the southern states where the price of a good negro was higher than in Kentucky. When he reached Louisville he was offered a good price for her service and hired her out to cook at a hotel. John grieved over the loss of his mother but afterwards learned she had been well treated at Louisville. John Rudd continued to work for Henry Moore until the Civil War ended. Then Henry Snyder came to the Moore home and demanded his brothers to be given into his charge.

Henry Snyder had enlisted in the Federal Army and had fought throughout the war. He had entered or leased seven acres of good land seven miles below Owensboro, Kentucky, and on those good acres of Davies County farm land the mother and her three sons were reunited.

John Rudd had never seen a river until he made the trip to Owensboro with his brother Henry. The trip was made on the big Gray Eagle and Uncle John declares "I was sure thrilled to get that boat ride." He relates many incidents of run-away Negroes. Remembers his fear of the Ku Klucks, and remembers seeing seven ex-slaves hanging from one tree near the top of Grimes-Hill, just after the close of the war.

When John grew to young manhood he worked on farms in Davis County near Owensboro for several years, then procured the job of portering for John Sporree, a hotel keeper at Owensboro, and in this position John worked for fifteen years.

While at Owensboro he met the trains and boats. He recalls the boats; Morning Star, and Guiding Star; both excursion boats that carried gay men and women on pleasure trips up and down the Ohio river.

Uncle John married Teena Queen his beloved first wife, at Owensboro. To this union was born one son but he has not been to see his father nor has he heard from him for thirty years, and his father believes him to have died. The second wife was Minnie Dixon who still lives with Uncle John at Evansville.

When asked what his political ideas were, Uncle John said his politics is his love for his government. He draws an old age compensation of 14 dollars a month.

Uncle John had some trouble proving his age but met the situation by having a friend write to the Catholic Church authorities at Springfield. Mrs. Simms had taken the position of God Mother to the baby and his birth and christening had been recorded in the church records. He is a devout Catholic and believes that religion and freedom are the two richest blessings ever given to mankind.

Uncle John worked as janitor at the Boehne Tuberculosis Hospital for eight years. While working there he received a fall which crippled him. He walks by the aid of a cane but is able to visit with his friends and do a small amount of work in his home.

Federal Writers' Project
of the W.P.A.
District #6
Marion County
Anna Pritchett
1200 Kentucky Avenue, Indianapolis, Indiana

FOLKLORE
AMANDA ELIZABETH SAMUELS
1721 Park Avenue

AMANDA ELIZABETH SAMUELS

Lizzie was a child in the home of grandma and grandpa McMurry. They were farmers in Robinson County, Tennessee.

Her mother, a slave hand, worked on the farm until her young master, Robert McMurry was married. She was then sold to Rev. Carter Plaster and taken to Logan County, Kentucky.

The child, Lizzie was given to young Robert. She lived in the house to help the young mistress who was not so kind to her. Lizzie was forced to eat chicken heads, fish heads, pig tails, and parsnips. The child disliked this very much, and was very unhappy with her young mistress, because in Robert's father's home all slave children were treated just like his own children. They had plenty of good substantial food, and were protected in every way.

The old master felt they were the hands of the next

generation and if they were strong and healthy, they would bring in a larger amount of money when sold.

Lizzie's hardships did not last long as they were set free soon after young Robert's marriage. He took her in a wagon to Keysburg, Kentucky to be with her mother.

Lizzie learned this song from the soldiers.

Old Saul Crawford is dead,
And the last word is said.
They were fond of looking back
Till they heard the bushes crack
And sent them to their happy home
In Cannan.
Some wears worsted
Some wears lawn
What they gonna do
When that's all gone.

Interviewer's Comment

Mrs. Samuels is an amusing little woman, she must be about 80 years old, but holds to the age of 60. Had she given her right age, the people for whom she works would have helped her to get her pension.

They are amused, yet provoked because Lizzie wants to be younger than she really is.

Submitted December 1, 1937
Indianapolis, Indiana

G. Monroe
Dist. 4
Jefferson County

SLAVE STORY
MR. JACK SIMMS' STORY

MR. JACK SIMMS

Personal Interview

Mr. Simms was born and raised on Mill Creek Kentucky, and now lives in Madison Indiana on Poplar Street diagonally North West of the hospital.

He was so young he did no remember very much about how the slaves were treated, but seemed to regret very much that he had been denied the privilege of an education. Mr. Simms remembers seeing the lines of soldiers on the Campbellsburg road, but referred to the war as the "Revolution War".

This was a very interesting old man, when we first called, his daughter invited us into the house, but her father wanted to talk outside where he "spit better". When his daughter conveyed this information Mr. Simms' immediately decided that we could come in as we "wouldn't be there long anyhow".

After we gained entrance, the daughter remarked that her father was very young at the time of the war, whereupon he answered very testily "If you are going to tell it, go ahead. Or am I going to tell it?"

Beulah Van Meter
District 4
Clark County

BILLY SLAUGHTER
1123 Watt St.
Jeffersonville

BILLY SLAUGHTER

Billy Slaughter was born Sept. 15, 1858, on the Lincoln Farm near Hodgenville, Ky. The Slaughters who now live between the Dixie Highway and Hodgenville on the right of the road driving toward Hodgenville about four miles off the state highway are the descendants of the old slave's master. This old slave was sold once and was given away once before he was given his freedom.

The spring on the Lincoln Farm that falls from a cliff was a place associated with Indian cruelty. It was here in the pool of water below the cliff that the Indians would throw babies of the settlers. If the little children could swim or the settlers could rescue them they escaped, otherwise they were drowned. The Indians would gather around the scene of the tragedy and rejoice in their fashion. The old slave when he was a baby was thrown in this pool but was rescued by white people. He remembers having seen several Indians but not many.

The most interesting subject that Billy Slaughter discussed was the Civil War. This was ordinarily believed to be fought over slavery, but it really was not, according to his interpretation, which is unusual for an old slave to state. The real reason was that the South withdrew from the Union and elected Jefferson Davis President of the Confederacy. In his own dialect he narrated these events accurately. The southerners or Democrats were called "Rebels" and "Secess" and the Republicans were called "Abolitionists."

Another point of interest was John Brown and Harpers Ferry. When Harper's Ferry was fired upon, that was firing upon the United States. It was here and through John Brown's Raid that war was virtually declared. The old Negro explained that Brown was an Abolitionist, and was captured here and later killed. While the old slave had the utmost respect for the Federal Government he regarded John Brown as a martyr for the cause of freedom and included him among the heroes he worshipped. Among his prized possessions is an old book written about John Brown's Raid.

The old slave's real hero was Abraham Lincoln. He plans another pilgrimage to the Lincoln Farm to look again at the cabin in which his Emancipator was born. He asked me if I read history very much. I assured him that I read it to some extent. After that he asked me if I recalled reading about Lincoln during the Civil War walking the White House floor one night and a Negro named Douglas remained in his presence. In the beginning of the War the Negroes who enlisted in the Union Army were given freedom, also the wives, and the children who were not married.

Another problem that was facing the North at this time was that the men who were taken from the farm and factory to the army could not be replaced by the slaves and production continued in the North as was being done in the south. Not all Negroes who wanted to join the Union forces were able to do so because of the strict watchfulness of their masters. The slaves were made to fight in the southern army whether they wanted to or not. This lessened the number of free Negroes in the Northern army. As a result Lincoln decided to free all Negroes. That was the decision he made the night he walked the White House floor. This was the old darkey's story of the conditions that brought about the Emancipation Proclamation. Freeing the Negroes was brought about during the Civil War but it was not the reason that the war was fought, was the unusual opinion of this Negro. "Uncle Billy's" father joined the Union army at the Taylor Barracks, near Louisville, Ky., which was the Camp Taylor during the World War. Uncle Billy's father and mother and their children who were not married were given freedom. The old slave has kept the papers that were drawn up for this act.

The old darkey explained that the Negro soldiers never fought in any decisive battles. There must always be someone to clean and polish the harness, care for the horses, dig ditches, and construct parapets. This slave's father was at Memphis during the battle there.

The Slaughter family migrated to Jeffersonville in '65. Billy was then seven years old. At that time there was only one depot here—a freight and passenger depot at Court and Wall Streets. What is now known as Eleventh St. was then a hickory grove—a paradise for squirrel hunters. On the ridge beginning at 7th and Mechanic Sts. were persimmon trees. This was a splendid hunting haven for the Negroes for their favorite wild animal—the o'possum. The ridge is known today as 'Possum Ridge. The section east of St. Anthony's Cemetery was covered in woods. Since there were a number of Beechnuts, pigeons frequented this place and were sought here. One could catch them faster than he could shoot them.

At this time there were two shipyards in Jeffersonville—Barmore's and Howard's. Barmore's shipyard location was first the location of a big meat-packing company. The old darkey called it a "pork house".

The old slave had seen several boats launched from these yards. Great crowds would gather for this event. After the hull was completed in the docks the boat was ready to launch. The blocks that served as props were knocked down one at a time. One man would knock down each prop. There were several men employed in this work on the appointed day of the launching of the boat. The boat would be christened with a bottle of champagne on its way to the river.

"Uncle Billy" worked on a steamboat in his earlier days. This boat traveled from Louisville to New Orleans. People traveled on the river for there were few railroads. The first work the old darkey did was to clean the decks. Later he cleaned up inside the boat, mopped up the floors and made the berths. The next job he held was ladies' cabin man. Later he took care of the quarters where the officials of the boat slept. The darkey also worked as a second pantry man. This work consisted of waiting on the tables in the dining room. The men's clothes had to be spotless. Sometimes it would become necessary for him to change his shirt three times a day.

The meats on the menu would include pigeon, duck, turkey, chicken, quail, beef, pork, and mutton. Vegetables of the season were served, as well as desserts. It was nothing unusual for a half dollar to be left under a plate as a tip for the waiter. Those who worked in the cabins never set a price for a shoe shine. Fifteen cents was the lowest they ever received.

During a yellow fever epidemic before a quarantine could be declared a boatload of three hundred people left Louisville at night to go to Memphis, Tenn. During the same time this boat went to New Orleans where yellow fever was raging. The captain warned them of it. In two narrow streets the old darkey recalled how he had seen the people fall over dead. These streets were crowded and there were no sidewalks, only room for a wagon. Here the victims would be sitting in the doorways, apparently asleep, only to fall over dead.

When the boat returned, one of the crew was stricken with this disease. Uncle Billy nursed him until they reached his home at Cairo, Ill. No one else took the yellow fever and this man recovered.

Another job "Uncle Billy" held was helping to make the brick used in the U.S. Quarter Master Depot. Colonel James Keigwin operated a brick kiln in what is now a colored settlement between 10th and 14th and Watt and Spring Sts. The clay was obtained from this field. It was his task to off-bare the brick after they were taken from the molds, and to place them in the eyes to be burned. Wood was used as fuel.

"Uncle Billy" reads his Bible quite often. He sometimes wonders why he is still left here—all of his friends are gone; all his brothers and sisters are gone. But this he believes is the solution—that there must be someone left to tell about old times.

"The Bible," he quotes, "says that two shall be working in the field together and one shall be taken and the other left. I am the one who is left," he concludes.

Henrietta Karwowski, Field Worker
Federal Writers' Project
St. Joseph County—District #1
South Bend, Indiana

EX-SLAVES
MR. AND MRS. ALEX SMITH
127 North Lake Street
South Bend, Indiana

MR. AND MRS. ALEX SMITH

Mr. and Mrs. Alex Smith, an eighty-three year old negro couple were slaves in Kentucky near Paris, Tennessee, as children. They now reside at 127 North Lake Street, on the western limits of South Bend. This couple lives in a little shack patched up with tar paper, tin, and wood.

Mrs. Elizabeth Smith, the talkative member or the family is a small woman, very wrinkled, with a stocking cap pulled over her gray hair. She wore a dress made of three different print materials; sleeves of one kind, collar of another and body of a third. Her front teeth were discolored, brown stubs, which suggested that she chews tobacco.

Mr. Alex Smith, the husband is tall, though probably he was a well built man at one time. He gets around by means of a cane. Mrs. Smith said that he is not at all well, and he was in the hospital for six weeks last winter.

The wife, Elizabeth or Betty, as her husband calls her,

was a slave on the Peter Stubblefield plantation in Kentucky, the nearest town being Paris, Tennessee, while Mr. Smith was a slave on the Robert Stubblefield plantation nearby.

Although only a child of five, Mr. Smith remembers the Civil War, especially the marching of thousands of soldiers, and the horse-drawn artillery wagons. The Stubblefields freed their slaves the first winter after the war.

On the Peter Stubblefield plantation the slaves were treated very well and had plenty to eat, while on the Robert Stubblefield plantation Mr Smith went hungry many times, and said, "Often, I would see a dog with a bit of bread, and I would have been willing to take it from him if I had not been afraid the dog would bite me."

Mrs. Smith was named after Elizabeth Stubblefield, a relative of Peter Stubblefield. As a child of five years or less, Elizabeth had to spin "long reels five cuts a day," pick seed from cotton, and cockle burrs from wool, and perform the duties of a house girl.

Unlike the chores of Elizabeth, Mr. Smith had to chop wood, carry water, chop weeds, care for cows, pick bugs from tobacco plants. This little boy had to go barefoot both summer and winter, and remembers the cracking of ice under his bare feet.

The day the mistress and master came and told the slaves they were free to go any place they desired, Mrs. Smith's mother told her later that she was glad to be free but she had no place to go or any money to go with. Many of the slaves would not leave and she never witnessed such crying as went on. Later Mrs. Smith was paid for working. She worked in the fields for "wittels" and clothes. A few years later she nursed children for twenty-five cents a week and "wittels," but after a time she received fifty cents a week, board and two dresses. She married Mr. Smith at the age of twenty.

Mr Smith's father rented a farm and Mr. Smith has been a farmer all his life. The Smith couple have been married sixty-four years. Mrs. Smith says, "and never a cross word exchanged. Mr. Smith and I had no children."

The room the writer was invited into was a combination bed-room and living room with a large heating stove in the centre of the small room. A bed on one side, a few chairs about the room. The floor was covered with an old patched rug. The only other room beside this room was a very small kitchen. The whole home was shabby and poor.

The only means of support the family has is a government old age pension which amounts to about fourteen dollars a month.

Their little shack is situated in the center of a large lot around which a very nice vegetable garden is planted. The property belongs to Mr. Harry Brazy, and the old couple does not pay rent or taxes and they may stay there as long as they live, "which is good enough for us," says Mrs. Smith.

As the writer was leaving Mrs. Smith said, "I like to talk and meet people. Come again."

Robert C. Irvin
District #2
Noblesville, Ind.

EX-SLAVE, LIFE STORY OF
BARNEY STONE, FORMER SLAVE, HAMILTON CO.

BARNEY STONE

This is the life story of Barney Stone, a highly re-spected colored gentleman of Noblesville, Hamil-ton County seat. Mr. Stone is near nintey-one years old, is in sound physical condition and still has a remark-able memory. He was a slave in the state of Kentucky for more than sixteen years and a soldier in the Union army for nearly two years. He educated himself and taught school to colored children four years following the Civil War. He studied in 1868, and has been a preacher in the Colored Baptist Faith for sixty nine years, having been instrumental in the building of seven churches in that time. Mr. Stone joined the K. of P. Lodge, the I.O.O.F. and Masonic Lodge and is still a member of the latter.

This fine old colored man has always worked hard for the uplift and advancement of the colored race and has accomplished much in this effort in the States of Tennes-see, Kentucky and Indiana. He, together with his preach-ing of the gospel, and his lecturing, has followed farming. He now has a field of sweet corn and a fine, large garden, which he plowed, planted and tended himself and not a weed can be found in either. He is the only ex-slave now living in Hamilton County, the others all deceased, and is one of three living members of Hamilton county G.A.R. the other two members being white.

Mr. Stone has given to the writer "My Life's Story", which he desires to call it, and in this story he pictures to the reader, "sixteen years of hell as a slave on a plantation," a story which will convince the reader that, even though much blood was shed in our Civil War, the war was a Godsend to the American Nation. This story is told just as given by Mr. Stone.

MY LIFE'S STORY

"My name is Barney Stone, I was born in slavery, May 17, 1847, in Spencer County, Kentucky. I was a slave on the plantation of Lemuel Stone (all slaves bore the last name of their master) for nearly seventeen years and was considered a leader among the young slaves on our plantation. My Mammy was mother to ten children, all slaves, and my Pappy, Buck Grant, was a buck slave on the plantation of John Grant, his Mastah; my pappy was used much as a male cow is used on the stock farm and was hired out to other plantation owners for that purpose and was regarded as a valuable slave. His Mastah permitted him to visit my mother each week-end on our plantation.

My Mastah was a hard man when he was angry, drinking or not feeling well, then at times he was kind to us. I was compelled to pick cotton and do other work when I was a very small boy. Mastah would never sell me because I was regarded as the best young slave on the plantation. Different from many other slaves, I was kept on the plantation from the day I was born until the day I ran away.

Slaves were sold in two ways, sometimes at private sale to a man who went about the Southland buying slaves until he has many in his possession, then he would have a big auction sale and would re-sell them to the highest bidder, much in the same manner as our live-stock are sold now in auction sales. Professional slave buyers in those days were called "nigger buyers". He came to the plantation with a doctor. He would point out two or three slaves which looked good to him and which could be spared by the owner, and would have the doctor examine the slave's heart. If the doctor pronounced the slave as sound, then the nigger buyer would make an offer to the owner and if the amount was satisfactory, the slave was sold. Some large plantation owners, having a large number of slaves, would hold a public auction and dispose of some of them, then he would attend another sale and buy new slaves, this was done sometimes to get better slaves and sometimes to make money on the sale of them.

Many times, as I have said before, our treatment on our plantation was horrible. When I was just a small boy, I witnessed my sister sold and taken away. One day one of horses came into the barn and Mastah noticed that she was caripped. He flew into a rage and thought I had hurt the horse, either that, or that I knew who did it. I told him that I did not do it and he demanded that I tell him who did it, if I didn't. I did not know and when I told him so, he secured a whip tied me to a post and whipped me until I was covered with blood. I begged him, "Mastah, Mastah, please don't whip me, I do not know who did it." He then took out his pocket knife and I would have been killed if

Missus (his dear wife) had not make him quit. She untied me and cared for me.

Many has been the time, I have seen my mammy beaten mercilessly and for no good reason. One day, not long before the out-break of the Civil War, a nigger buyer came and I witnessed my dear Mammy and my one year old baby brother, sold. I seen er taken away, never to see her again until I found her twenty-seven years later at Clarksburg, Tennessee. My baby brother was with her, but I did not know him until Mammy told me who he was, he had grown into a large man. That was a happy meeting. After those experiences of "sixteen long years in hell, as a slave", I was very bitter against the white man, until after I ran away and joined the Union army.

At the out-break of the Civil War and when the Northern army was marching into the Southland, hundreds of male slaves were shot down by the Rebels, rather than see them join with the Yankees. One day when I learned that the Northern troops were very close to our plantation, I ran away and hid in a culvert, but was found and I would have been shot had the Yankee troops not scattered them and that saved me. I joined that Union army and served one year, eight months and twenty-two days, and fought with them in the battle of Fort Wagnor, and also in the battle of Milikin's Bend. When I went into the army, I could not read or write. The white soldiers took an interest in me and taught me to write and read, and when the war was over I could write a very good letter. I taught what little I knew to colored children after the War.

I studied day and night for the next three years at the home of a lawyer, educating myself and in 1868, I start-

ed preaching the gospel of Jesus Christ and have continued to do so for sixty-nine years. In that time I have
been instrumental in the building of seven churches in
Kentucky, Tennessee and Indiana. I did this good work
through gratefulness to God for my deliverance and my
salvation. During my life, I have joined the K. of P. Lodge,
and I.O.O.F and Masonic Lodge. I have preached for the
up-life and advancement of the colored races. I have accomplished much good in this life and have raised a family of eight children. I love and am loyal to my country
and have received great compensation from my government for my services. I am in good health and still able
to work, and I am thankful to my God and my country."

Stories from Ex-Slaves
5th District
Vanderburgh County
Lauana Creel
1415 S. Barker Avenue, Evansville, Indiana

ESCAPE FROM BONDAGE OF ADAH ISABELLE SUGGS

ADAH ISABELLE SUGGS

Among the interesting stories connected with former slaves one of the most outstanding ones is the life story of Adah Isabelle Suggs, indeed her escape from slavery planned and executed by her anxious mother, Harriott McClain, bears the earmarks of fiction, but the truth of all related occurences has been established by the aged negro woman and her daughter Mrs. Harriott Holloway, both citizens of Evansville, Indiana.

Born in slavery before January the twenty-second, 1862 the child Adah McClain was the property of Colonel Jackson McClain and Louisa, his wife.

According to the customary practice of raising slave children, Adah was left at the negro quarters of the McClain plantation, a large estate located in Henderson county, three and one half miles from the village of Henderson, Kentucky. There she was cared for by her mother. She retains many impressions gained in early childhood of the slave quarters; she remembers the slaves singing and dancing together after the day of toil. Their voices were strong and their songs were sweet. "Master was good to his slaves and never beat them" were her words concerning her master.

When Adah was not yet five years of age the mistress, Louisa McClain, made a trip to the slave quarters to review conditions of the negroes. It was there she discovered that one little girl there had been developing ideas and ideals; the mother had taught the little one to knit tiny stockings, using wheat straws for knitting needles.

Mrs. McClain at once took charge of the child taking her from her mother's care and establishing her room at the residence of the McClain family.

Today the aged Negro woman recalls the words of praise and encouragement accorded her accomplishments, for the child was apt, active, responsive to influence and soon learned to fetch any needed volume from the library shelves of the McClain home.

She was contented and happy but the mother knew that much unhappiness was in store for her young daughter if she remained as she was situated.

A custom prevailed throughout the southern states that the first born of each slave maiden should be the son or daughter of her master and the girls were forced into maternity at puberty. The mothers naturally resisted this terrible practice and Harriott was determined to prevent her child being victimized.

One planned escape was thwarted; when the girl was about twelve years of age the mother tried to take her to a place of safety but they were overtaken on the road to the ferry where they hoped to be put across the Ohio river.

They were carried back to the plantation and the mother was mildly punished and imprisoned in an upstair room.

The little girl knew her mother was imprisoned and often climbed up to a window where the two could talk together.

One night the mother received directions through a dream in which her escape was planned. She told the child about the dream and instructed her to carry out orders that they might escape together.

The girl brought a large knife from Mrs. McClain's pantry and by the aid of that tool the lock was pried from the prison door and the mother made her way into the open world about midnight.

A large tobacco barn became her refuge where she waited for her child. The girl had some trouble making her escape; she had become a useful and necessary member of her mistress' household and her services were hourly in demand. The Daughter "young missus" Annie McClain was afflicted from birth having a cleft palate and later developing heart dropsy which made regular surgery imperative. The negro girl had learned to care for the young white woman and could draw the bandages for the surgeon whey "Young Missus" underwent surgical treatment.

The memory of one trip to Louisville is vivid in the mind of the old negress today for she was taken to the city and the party stopped at the Gault House and [TR: line not completed]

"It was a grand place," she declares, as she describes the surroundings; the handsome draperies and the winding stairway and other artistic objects seen at the grand hotel.

The child loved her young mistress and the young mistress desired the good slave should be always near her; so, patient waiting was required by the negro mother before her daughter finally reached their rendezvous.

Under cover of night the two fugitives traveled the three miles to Henderson, there they secreted themselves under the house of Mrs. Margaret Bentley until darkness fell over the world to cover their retreat. Imagine the frightened negroes stealthily creeping through the woods in constant fear of being recaptured. Federal soldiers put them across the river at Henderson and from that point they cautiously advanced toward Evansville. The husband of Harriott, Milton McClain and her son Jerome were volunteers in a negro regiment. The operation of the Federal Statute providing for the enlistment of slaves made enlisted negroes free as well as their wives and children, so, by that statute Harriott McClain and her daughter should have been given their freedom.

When the refugees arrived in Evansville they were befriended by free negroes of the area. Harriott obtained a position as maid with the Parvine family, "Miss Hallie and Miss Genevieve Parvine were real good folks," declares the aged negro Adah when repeating her story. After working for the Misses Parvine for about two years, the negro mother had saved enough money to place her child in "pay school" there she learned rapidly.

Adah McClain was married to Thomas Suggs January 18, 1872. Thomas was a slave of Bill McClain and it is believed he adopted the name Suggs because a Mr. Suggs had befriended him in time of trouble. Of this fact neither the wife nor daughter have positive proof. The father has departed this life but Adah Suggs lives on with her memories.

Varied experiences have attended her way. Wifehood and devotion; motherhood and care she has known for she has given fifteen children to the world. Among them were one set of twins, daughters and triplets, two sons and a daughter. She is a beloved mother to those of her children who remain near her and says she is happy in her belief in God and Christ and hopes for a glorious hereafter where she can serve the Lord Jesus Christ and praise him eternally.

What greater hope can be given to the mortal than the hope cherished by Adah Isabelle Suggs?

Folklore
District #5
Vanderburgh County
Lauana Creel

"A TRADITION FROM PRE-CIVIL WAR DAYS"
KATIE SUTTON, AGED EX-SLAVE
Oak street, Evansville, Ind.

KATIE SUTTON

"**W**hite folks 'jes naturally different from dar-kies," said Aunt Katie Sutton, ex-slave, as she tightened her bonnet strings under her wrinkled chin.

"We's different in color, in talk and in ligion and be-liefs. We's different in every way and can never be spect-ed to think oe [TR: or?] to live alike."

"When I was a little gal I lived with my mother in an old log cabin. My mammy was good to me but she had to spend so much of her time at humoring the white babies and taking care of them that she hardly ever got to even sing her own babies to sleep."

"Ole Missus and Young Missus told the little slave children that the stork brought the white babies to their mothers but that the slave children were all hatched out from buzzards eggs and we believed it was true."

"Yes, Maam, I believes in evil spirits and that there are many folks that can put spells on you, and if'n you dont believe it you had better be careful for there are folks right here in this town that have the power to bewitch you and then you will never be happy again."

Aunt Katie declared that the seventh son of a seventh son, or the seventh daughter of a seventh daughter possesses the power to heal diseases and that a child born after the death of its father possesses a strange and unknown power.

While Aunt Katie was talking, a neighbor came in to borrow a shovel from her.

"No, no, indeed I never lends anything to nobody," she declared. After the new neighbor left, Aunt Katie said, "She jes erbout wanted dat shovel so she could 'hax' me. A woman borrowed a poker from my mammy and hexed mammy by bending the poker and mammy got all twisted up wid rhumatis 'twill her uncle straightened de poker and den mammy got as straight as anybody."

"No, Maam, nobody wginter take anything of mine out'n this house." Aunt Katie Sutton's voice was thin and her tune uncertain but she remembered some of the songs she heard in slavery days. One was a lullaby sung by her mother and the song is given on separate pages of this artical.

Three years ago Aunt Katie was called away on her last journey although she had always emmerced the back and front steps of her cottage with chamber lye daily to keep away evil spirits death crept in and demanded the price each of us must pay and Katie answered the call.

Aunt Katie sprinkled salt in the foot prints of departing guests "Dat's so dey kain leave no illwill behind em and can never come agin 'thout an invitation," she explained.

She said she one time planted a tree with a curse and that her worst enemy died that same year.

"Evil spirits creeps around all night long and evil people's always able to hex you, So, you had best be careful how you talks to strangers. Always spit on a coin before You gives it to a begger and dont pass too close to a hunchbacked person unless you can rub the hump or you will have bad luck as sure as anything."

Aunt Katie declared a rabbit's foot only brought good luck if the rabbit had been killed by a cross eyed negro in a country grave yard in the dark of the moon and she said that she believed one of that description could be found only once in a lifetime or possibly a hundred years.

"A Slave Mammy's Lullaby."

Sung by Katie Sutton, Ex-slave of Evansville, Indiana.

"A snow white stork flew down from the sky.
Rock a bye, my baby bye,
To take a baby gal so fair,
To young missus, waitin there;
When all was quiet as a mouse,
In ole massa's big fine house.

Refrain:
Dat little gal was borned rich and free,
She's de sap from out a sugah tree;
But you are jes as sweet to me;
My little colored chile,

Jes lay yo head upon my bres;
An res, and res, and res, an res,
My little colored chile.

To a cabin in a woodland drear,
You've come by a mammy's heart to cheer;
In this ole slave's cabin,
Your hands my heart strings grabbin;
Jes lay your head upon my bres,
Jes snuggle close an res an res;
My little colored chile.

Repeat Refrain.

Yo daddy ploughs ole massa's corn,
Yo mammy does the cooking;
She'll give dinner to her hungry chile,
When nobody is a lookin;
Don't be ashamed, my chile, I beg,
Case you was hatched from a buzzard's egg;
My little colored chile."

Repeat Refrain.

William R. Mays
Dist. No. 4
Johnson Co.
Aug. 2, 1937

SLAVERY DAYS OF GEORGE THOMPSON

GEORGE THOMPSON

My name is George Thompson, I was born in Monroe County, Kentucky near the Cumberland river Oct. 8, 1854, on the Manfred Furgeson plantation, who owned about 50 slaves. Mister Furgerson [TR: before, Furgeson] was a preacher and had three daughters and was kind to his slaves.

I was quite a small boy when our family, which included an older sister, was sold to Ed. Thompson in Medcalf Co. Kentucky, who owned about 50 other slaves, and as was the custom then we was given the name of our new master, "Thompson".

I was hardly twelve years old when slavery was abolished, yet I can remember at this late date most of the happenings as they existed at that time.

I was so young and unexperienced when freed I remained on the Thompson plantation for four years after the war and worked for my board and clothes as coach boy and any other odd jobs around the plantation.

I have no education, I can neither read nor write, as a slave I was not allowed to have books. On Sundays I would go into the woods and gather ginseng which I would sell to the doctors for from 10¢ to 15¢ a pound and with this money I would buy a book that was called the Blue Back Speller. Our master would not allow us to have any books and when we were lucky enough to own a book we would have to keep it hid, for if our master would find us with a book he would whip us and take the book from us. After receiving three severe whippings I gave up and never again tried for any learning, and to this day I can neither read nor write.

Slaves were never allowed off of their plantation without a written pass, and if caught away from their plantation without a pass by the Pady-Rollers or Gorillars (who were a band of ruffians) they wore whipped.

As there were no oil lamps or candles, another black boy and myself were stationed at the dining table to hold grease lamps for the white folks to see to eat. And we would use brushes to shoo away the flies.

In 1869 I left the plantation to go on my own. I landed in Heart County, Ky. and went to work for Mr. George Parish in the tobacco fields at $25.00 per year and two suits of clothes; after working two years for Mr. Parish I left. I drifted from place to place in Alabama and Mississippi, working first at one place and then another, and finally drifted into Franklin in 1912 and went to work on the Fred Murry farm on Hurricane road for 10 years. I afterwards worked for Ashy Furgerson, a house mover.

I have lived at my present address, 651 North Young St. since coming to Franklin.

(Can furnish photograph if wanted) [TR: no photo-graph found.]

Archie Koritz, Field Worker
Federal Writers' Project
Porter County—District #1
Valparaiso, Indiana

EX-SLAVES
REV. WAMBLE
1827 Madison Street
Gary, Indiana

[TR: above 'Wamble' in handwriting is 'Womble']

REV. WAMBLE

Rev. Wamble was born a slave in Monroe County, Mississippi, in 1859. The Westbrook family owned many slaves in charge of over-seers who managed the farm, on which there were usually two hundred or more slaves. One of the Westbrook daughters married a Mr. Wamble, a wagon-maker. The Westbrook family gave the newly-weds two slaves, as did the Wamble family. One of the two slaves coming from the Westbrook family was Rev. Wamble's grandfather. It seems that the slaves took the name of their master, hence Rev. Wamble's grandfather was named Wamble.

Families owning only a few slaves and in moderate circumstances usually treated their slaves kindly since like a farmer with only a few horses, it was to their best interest to see that their slaves were well provided for. The slaves were valuable, and there was no funds to buy others, whereas the large slave owners were wealthy and one slave more or less made little difference. The Reverend's father and his brothers were children of original African slaves and were of the same age as the Wamble boys and grew up together. The Reverend's grandfather was manager of the farm and the three Wamble boys worked under him the same as the slaves. Mr. Wamble never permitted any of his slaves to be whipped, nor were they mistreated.

Mr. Westbrook was a deacon in the Methodist Church and had two slave over-seers to manage the farm and the slaves. He was very severe with his slaves and none were ever permitted to leave the farm. If they did leave the farm and were found outside, they were arrested and whipped. Then Westbrook was notified and one of the over-seers would come and take the slave home where he would again be whipped. The slave was tied to a cedar tree or post and lashed with a snake whip.

Rev. Wamble's mother was a Deerbrook [HW: West-brook] slave and when the Reverend was two years of age, his mother died from a miscarriage caused by a whipping. When the women slaves were in an advanced stage of pregnancy they were made to lie face down in a specially dug depression in the ground and were whipped. Other-wise they were treated like the men. Their arms were tied around a cedar tree or post, and they were lashed.

Since the Reverend appeared to be a promising slave, both the Westbrooks and the Wambles wanted him, much like one would want a valuable colt today. Since the Reverend's grandmother was a Westbrook and the Wambles treated the slaves much better, she wanted him to become a Wamble. She hid the child in a shed, what would probably be a poor dog-house today, and fed the child during the night time.

During this period of his life the Reverend remembers what happened to one of the Westbrook slaves who had run away. One evening he came to the Wamble home and asked for some supper. Wamble took the slave into his home and after feeding him, placed a log chain which was hanging above the fire-place, around the slave's waist, left him to sleep on a bench in front of the fire-place. The next morning after the slave was given breakfast by the Wambles, Westbrook, his son and over-seer appeared. Rev. Wamble in his hide-out remembers being awakened by the sound of the slave being whipped and the moaning of the slave. After the whipping, the slave was turned loose. After he had gone about a mile through the bottom-land toward the river, Westbrook turned his hounds loose on the slave's tracks. The hounds treed the slave before he had gone another mile, much like a dog would tree a cat.

The Westbrooks pulled the slave down from the tree and the dogs slashed his foot. The slave was then whipped and long ropes placed around him. He was driven back to the Wamble place with whips where he was once again whipped. They [TR: Then?] they drove him two miles to the Westbrook place where he was whipped once more. Whatever became of the slave, whether he died or recovered, is unknown. One unusual feature of this story is that Westbrook who permitted his slaves to be whipped, was a church deacon, whereas Wamble, who never attended church, never whipped or mistreated his slaves.

The Reverend states that in the community where he resided the slaves were well treated except for the whippings they received. They were well-fed, and if injured or sick, were attended by a doctor on the same principal that a person would care for an injured horse or sick cow. The slaves were valuable, and it was to the best interest of the owner to see that they were able to work.

In case of slaves having children, the children became the property of the mother's owner. If the south had won the war, Wamble would have been a Westbrook since his mother was a Westbrook slave, and if it lost, he would go to live with his father and take the name of his father, a Wamble slave. So until the war was over he was hid out much like a small child would bring a stray dog home and hide it somewhere for fear that if his parents discovered it, it would be taken away.

The living quarters of the slaves were made of logs covered with mud, and the roof was covered with coarse boards upon which dirt about a foot in depth was placed. There were no floors except dirt or the bare ground. The furniture consisted of a small stove and the beds were two boards extending from two walls, the extending ends resting on a peg driven into the ground. This would make a one-legged bed. The two boards were covered across ways with more boards and the slaves slept on these boards or upon the dirt floor. There were no blankets provided for them. For food the slaves received plenty of meat, potatoes, and whatever could be raised. If the master had plenty to eat, so did the slaves, but if food was not plentiful for the master, the slaves had less to eat.

Only one of the three Wamble boys joined the southern army. Until the war was over, the other two boys who refused to go to war hid out in the surrounding woods and hills. The only time the Reverend's father left the farm was to attend his master Billy, when he was in a hospital recovering from wounds received in battle.

Wamble was a wagon-maker, and he made two or three wagons which usually took about six months. Then he hitched teams to them and went north to Missouri, Kansas and Arkansas and kept going until he had sold the wagons and teams, keeping one wagon and team, with which to return home. Some times the master would be gone for a period of nine to twelve months. During his absence the Reverend's grandfather was in charge of the farm.

The grandmother of Rev. Wamble was a full-blooded African negro, brought to this country as a slave at seventeen years of age. She was a very large and strong woman and was often hired out to do a man's work. Slaves were forbidden to have papers in their possession and since they were forbidden to read papers, hardly any slaves could read or write. There never was any occasion or need to do these things. It was not known that the Reverend's grandmother could read and write until after the Civil War. The Reverend remembers his grandmother bringing an old newspaper to his hide-out during the Civil War, late at night, after the Wamble family had retired, and making a candle from fried meat grease and a cord string, which made a very tiny light. She placed some old blankets over the walls so that no light could be seen through the cracks in the hut. She would then place the paper as near as possible to the light, without burning it, and read the paper. It was never discovered where or how she learned to read and write.

If a young, good-looking, husky negro was trustworthy, the family would make him the driver of the family carriage. They would dress him in the best clothes obtainable and with a silk-finished beaver skin hat. The driver sat on a seat on the top and towards the front of the carriage. He was compelled to stay on this seat when waiting for any of the family that he might be driving, regardless of the weather or the length of time that he had to wait.

The mail was carried in the same kind of vehicle with negro drivers. In each town there was a certain rack at which this mail carriage would stop in each village or wherever the designated stop was made. Upon nearing the rack and coming to a stop, the driver would blow a bugle call which could be heard for miles around, and people hearing this bugle would come and get their mail. The Reverend remembers that several of these drivers froze to death during the cold weather, and that in the winter, many times the horses on the mail carriage upon coming to this rack would stop, and the driver would be sitting frozen to death in his seat.

Men would take him down, carefully saving the silk beaver-skin hat for some other driver.

Since the slaves had no votes, they had no interest in politics when they became free and knew nothing about political conditions other than that after the Civil War they were free and had a vote. As a boy the Reverend re-members seeing the white and black soldiers marching on election day.

The politicians would always tell the negroes what was good for them and making it appear that it was for their best interest, and they should vote for him, always giving them the desert first and making them think that they were on the level no matter what the meal might be or what hardships they were causing the negro to suffer. On one instance after the negroes were forbidden to vote they marched in a body to the polls and demanded a Democratic ballot and were then permitted to vote.

Rev. Wamble was twenty-seven years of age before he saw and read his first newspaper. He lived with the Wambles for twenty years after the war, when his father then in partnership with another man, purchased forty acres of land. He attended his first school for a period of two months only in 1871. In 1872 the government built a school on his father's farm and it was taught by a missionary. The school term was for a period of three months each year. The Reverend attended this school for seven years.

In 1880 he married the first time. His first wife died in Memphis, Tennessee, in 1888. By this marriage there were four children. On February 1, 1892, the Reverend with his two surviving children all entered school at a college in Little Rock, Arkansas. One of his daughters died in the third year of her school year, but the other graduated from the Normal School and was a teacher for several years. At the present time she is married to a minister in Louisiana and is the mother of ten children and is a nurse. The three oldest children have degrees and the others are expected to do the same.

The Reverend married his second wife in 1894. She died in 1907. By this marriage nine children were born.

The Reverend has been in the ministry for thirty-seven years. Seeing the need of making more money, two of his sons came to Gary, Indiana, to work in 1924. Now both are working in the post-office. Two years later he came to Gary for the same reason and after working two years in the coke plant, was laid off due to the depression. The youngest daughter of the Reverend by his second marriage graduated from a college in Pine Bluff, Arkansas, and is now teaching in New York City.

Although the Reverend is advanced in years, he is quite active and healthy. He says he has a small pension and is just waiting until it is time to pass on to the next world. He has six children and seventeen grandchildren living.

As the Reverend remembered the south, none of the white people worked at manual labor, but usually sat under a shade tree. They were usually clerks, bookkeepers or tradesmen.

Ex-Slave Stories
5th District
Vanderburgh County
Lauana Creel
1415 S. Barker Avenue, Evansville, Indiana

THE BIOGRAPHY OF A CHILD BORN IN SLAVERY
SAMUEL WATSON
[HW: Personal Interview]

SAMUEL WATSON

S amuel Watson, a citizen of Evansville, Indiana, was born in Webster County, Kentucky, February 14, 1862. His master's home was located two and one half miles from Clay, Kentucky on Craborchard Creek.

"Uncle Sammy" as the negro children living near his home on South East Fifth Street call the old man, possesses an unusually clear memory. In fact he remembers seeing the soldiers and hearing the report of cannon while he was yet an infant.

One story told by the old negro relates how; "old missus" saved "old massa's horses". The story follows:

The mistress accompanied by a number of slaves was walking out one morning and all were startled by the sound of hurrying horses. Soon many mounted soldiers could be seen coming over a hill in the distance. The child Samuel was later told that the soldiers were making their way to Fort Donelson and were pressing horses into service. They were also enlisting negroes into service whenever possible.

Old master, Thomas Watson, owned many good able-bodied slaves and many splendid horses. The mistress realised the danger of loss and opening the "big gate" that separated the corral from the forest lands, Mrs. Watson ran into the midst of the horses shouting and frailing them. The frightened horses ran into the forest off the highway and toward the river.

When the soldiers stopped at the Watson plantation they found only a few old work horses standing under a tree and not desiring these they want on their way.

The little negro boy ran and hid himself in the corner made by a great outside chimney, where he was found later, by his frightened mother. Uncle Samuel remembers that the horses came home the following afternoon, none missing.

Uncle Samuel remembers when the war ended and the slaves were emancipated. "Some were happy! and some were sad!" Many dreaded leaving their old homes and their masters' families.

Uncle Samuel's mother and three children were told that they were free people and the master asked the mother to take her little ones and go away.

She complied and took her family to the plantation of Jourdain James, hoping to work and keep her family together. Wages received for her work failed to support the mother and children so she left the employ of Mr. James and worked from place to place until her children became half starved and without clothing.

The older children, remembering better and happier days, ran away from their mother and went back to their old master.

Thomas Watson went to Dixon, Kentucky and had an article of indenture drawn up binding both Thomas and Laurah to his service for a long number of years. Little Samuel only remained with his mother who took him to the home of William Allen Price. Mr. Price's plantation was situated in Webster County, Kentucky about half-way between Providence and Clay on Craborchard Creek. Mr. Price had the little boy indentured to his service for a period of eighteen years. There the boy lived and worked on the plantation.

He said he had a good home among good people. His master gave him five real whippings within a period of fourteen years but Uncle Samuel believes he deserved every lash administered.

Uncle Samuel loved his master's family, he speaks of Miss Lena, Miss Lula, Master Jefferson and Master John and believes they are still alive. Their present home is at Cebra, Kentucky.

It was the custom for a slave indentured to a master to be given a fair education, a good horse, bridle, saddle and a suit of clothes for his years of toil, but Mr. Price did not believe the boy deserved the pay and refused to pay him. A lawyer friend sued in behalf of the Negro and received a judgement of $115.00 (one hundred and fifteen dollars). Eighteen dollars repaid the lawyer for his service and Samuel started out with $95.00 and his freedom.

Evansville became the home of Samuel Watson in

1882. The trip was made by train to Henderson then on transfer boat along the Ohio to Evansville.

The young negro man was impressed by the boat and crew and said he loved the town from the first glimpse.

Dr. Bacon, a prominent citizen living at Chandler Avenue and Second Street, employed Samuel as coachman. His next service was as house-man for Levi Igleheart, 1010 Upper Second Street. Mr. Igleheart grew to trust Samuel and gave him many privileges allowing him to care for horses and to manage business for the family.

Samuel was married in 1890. His wife was born in Evansville and knew nothing of slavery by birth or indenture.

Uncle Samuel was given a job at the Trinity Church, corner of Third and Chestnut Streets. Mr. Igleheart recommended him for the position. He received $30.00 per month for his services for a period of six years.

Mr. McNeely employed him for several years as janitor for lodges and secret orders. The old negro was also a paper hanger and wall cleaner and did well untill the panic seized him as it did others.

Uncle Samuel was entitled to an old age pension which he recieved from 1934 until 1935 but January 15th, 1936 something went wrong and the money was with held. Then uncle Samuel was sent to the poor house. Still he was not unhappy and did what he could to make others happy.

In 1936 he again applied and received the pension. $17.00 per month is paid for his upkeep, his only labor consists of tending a little garden and doing light chores. He lives with William Crosby on S.E. Fifth Street.

Iris L Cook
District #4
Floyd County

SLAVE STORY
STORY OF NANCY WHALLEN
924 Pearl St.
New Albany, Ind.

NANCY WHALLEN

N ancy Whallen is now about 81 years of age. She doesn't know exactly. She was about 5 year of age when Freedom was declared. Nancy was born and raised in Hart County near Hardinsburg, Kentucky. She is very hard to talk to as her memory is failing and she can not hear very well.

The little negro girl lived the usual life of a rural negro in Civil War Time and afterwards. She remembers the "sojers" coming thru the place and asking for food. Some of them camped on the farm and talked to her and teased her.

She tells about one big nigger called "Scott" on the place who could outwork all the others. He would hang his hat and shirt on a tree limb and work all day long in the blazing sun on the hottest day.

The colored folk, used to have revivals, out in the woods. They would sometimes build a sort of brush shelter with leaves for a roof and service a would be held here. Preachin' and shouting' sometimes lasted all day Sundays. Colored folks came from miles around when they possibly could get away. These affairs were usually held away from the "white folks" who seldom if ever saw these gatherings.

Observation of the writer.

The old woman remembers the Big Eclipse of the sun or the "Day of Dark" as she called it. The chickens all went to roost and the darkies all thought the end of the world had come. The cattle lowed and everyone was scared to death.

She lived down in Kentucky after the War until she was quite a young woman and then came to Indiana where she has lived ever since. She lives now with her daughter in New Albany.

Special Assignment
Emily Hobson
Dist. #3
Parke County

INTERVIEW WITH ANDERSON WHITTED,
COLORED EX-SLAVE, OF ROCKVILLE, INDIANA

ANDERSON WHITTED

Mr. Whitted will be 89 years old next month October 1937. He was born in Orange County, North Carolina. His mother took care of the white children so her nine children were very well treated. The master was a Doctor. The family were Hickory Quakers and did not believe in mistreating their slaves, always providing them with plenty to eat, and clothing to wear to church on Sunday. Despite a law that prohibited books to Negroes, his family had a Bible, and an elementary spelling book. Mr. Whitted's father belonged to his master's half-brother and lived fourteen miles away. He was allowed a horse to go see them every two weeks. The father could read, and spell very well so would teach them on his visits. Mr. Whitted learned to read the Bible first, then in later years has learned to read other things. It was the custom for the master to search the negro huts, but Mr. Whitted's master never did.

The Doctor often took Mr. Whitted's grandmother with him to help care for the sick. When the war broke out the Master's son joined the southern forces. The son was wounded. The Doctor and Mr. Whitted's grandmother went for the boy. On the way home the Doctor died but the grandmother got the boy home and nursed him back to health. Life for the Negroes was different after the son began running the place, he was not good to them. Mr. Whitted was then 16 years old, and the older brother was the overseer. The negroes had been allowed a share of the crop but the new master refused them anything to live on. In that region the wheat was harvested the middle of June. There was a big crop that year but the entire family was turned out before the harvest, with nothing. Mr. Whitted left his older brother with his mother and the children sitting by the road, while he ran the 14 miles for his father to find out what to do. The father borrowed two teams and wagons, rented a house in the edge of town, and moved the family in.

The slaves were freed about that time, and for the first time in their lives they were free, and the entire family together. The father went to the governor for food. The government was allowing hard tack and pickled beef for the negroes. They received their allotment, and were well satisfied with hard tack because they were free. In telling about the pickled beef he says he never has seen any beef since that looked like it; he believed that it was horse meat. The father started working in a mill in 1865. He was soon bringing home food stuff from there, and in time they had a crop on their little place.

The older brother worked in the mornings and went to a Quaker Normal School in the afternoon. Pres. Harrison gave him an appointment in the revenue department, then as he grew older he was transferred to the post office department. He was retired on a pension at the age of 75. He is still living in Washington, D.C., and is now 97 years old.

During the war Mr. Whitted ran away, going 12 miles to the camp of the northern soldiers where he stayed two weeks. They gave him a horse to ride, and sent him gathering fuel through the woods for them. Those were the happiest days he had ever known—his first freedom.

Mr. Whitted was never sold, but he often saw processions go past after a sale, the wagon loaded with provisions first, then the slaves tied together following. They often took the babies away from their mothers, and sold them. Some old woman, too old to work, would then care for the little ones until they were old enough to work. At six years old they were put to work thinning corn, worming the tobacco, and pulling weeds. At seven they were taught to use a hoe. At 16 they were full hands, working along with the older men.

In April 1880 Mr. Whitted left Orange County, it was

so very rough it was hard to make a living. He just started out in search of a better place, leaving his wife and seven children there. In November he sent for them, he was working at the brick yards in Rockville. They were finishing the court house. He was so anxious to make a living he often did as much as two men. One child was born here. His wife died soon after coming to Rockville. He stayed single for three years, but found he could not care for his family and married again. His second wife died a number of years ago. He now spends the winters with his three living daughters, and during the summer months, a daughter comes to Rockville to enjoy his home.

Mr. Whitted's uncle belonged to a mean master. The slaves worked hard all day, then were chained together at night. The uncle ran away in the early part of the war, and after two years broke through the lines, and joined the northern army, going back after emancipation.

Iris Cook
Dist 4
Floyd Co.

SLAVE STORY
THE STORY OF ALEX WOODSON
905 E. 4th St.
New Albany, Ind.

ALEX WOODSON

Observation of Writer

Alex Woodson is an old light skinned darkey, he looks to be between 80 and 85, it is hard to tell his age, and colored folks hardly ever do know their correct age. I visited him in his little cottage and had a long talk with him and his wife (his second). "Planted the fust one." They run a little grocery in the front room of the cottage. But the stock was sadly run down. Together with the little store and his "pinshun" (old age pension) these old folks manage to get along.

Alex Woodson was born at Woodsonville, in Hart County, Kentucky, just across Green River from Munfordville. He was a good sized boy, possibly 7 years or more when "Freedom wuz declared". His master was "Old Marse" Sterrett who had about a 200 acre place and whose son in law Tom Williams ran a store on this place. When Williams married Sterretts daughter he was given Uncle Alex and his mother and brother as a present. Williams was then known as "Young Master."

When war come Old Master gave his (Woodson's) mother a big roll of bills, "greenbacks as big as Yo' arm", to keep for him, and was forced to leave the neighborhood. After the war the old darkey returned the money to him intact.

Uncle Alex remembers his mother taking him and other children and running down the river bank and hiding in the woods all night when the soldiers came. They were Morgan's men and took all available cattle and horses in the vicinity and beat the woods looking for Yankee soldiers. Uncle Alex said he saw Morgan at a distance on his big horse and he "wuz shore a mighty fine looker."

Sometimes the Yankee soldiers would come riding along and they "took things too".

When the War was over old Master came back home and the negroes continued to live on at the place as usual, except for a few that wanted to go North. Old Master lived in a great big house with all his family and the Negroes lived in another good sized house or quarters, all together. There were a few cabins.

"Barbecues! My we shore used to have 'em, yes ma'am, we did! Folks would come for miles around. Would roast whole hawgs and cows, and folks would sing, and eat and drink whiskey. The white folks had 'em but we helped and had fun too. Sometimes we would have one ourselves."

"Used to have rail splittin's and wood choppins. The men woud work all day, and get a pile of wood as big as a house. At noon they'd stop and eat a big meal that the women folks had fixed up for em. Them wuz some times, I've spent to many a one."

"I remember we used to go to revivals sometimes, down near Horse ave. Everybody got religion and we shore had some times. We don't have them kind of times any more. I remember I went back down to one of those revivals years afterwards. Most of the folks I used to know was dead or gone. The preacher made me set up front with him, and he asked me to preach to the folks. But I sez that "no, God hadn't made me that away and I wouldn't do it."

I've saw Abraham Lincoln's cabin many a time, when I was young. It set up on a high hill, and I've been to the spring under the hill lots of times. The house was on the Old National Road then. I hear they've fixed it all up now. I haven't been there for years.

After the war when I grewed up I married, and settled on the old place. I remember the only time I got beat in a horse trade. A sneakin' nigger from down near Horse Cave sold me a mule. That mule was jest natcherly no count. He would lay right down in the plow. One day after I had worked with him and tried to get him to work right, I got mad. I says to my wife, Belle, I'm goin' to get rid of that mule if I have to trade him for a cat. An' I led him off. When I came back I had another mule and $15 to boot. This mule she wuz shore skinny but when I fattened her up you wouldn't have known her."

"Finally I left the old place and we come north to Indiana. We settled here and I've been here for 50 years abourt. I worked in the old Rolling Mill. And I've been an officer in the Baptist Church at 3rd and Main for 41 years."

"Do I believe in ghosts" (Here his second wife gave a sniff) Well ma'am I don't believe in ghosts but I do in spirits. (another disgusted sniff from the second wife) I remember one time jest after my first wife died I was a sittin right in that chair your sittin in now. The front door opened and in come a big old grey mule, and I didn't have no grey mule. In she come just as easy like, put one foot down slow, and then the other, and then the other I says 'Mule git out here, you is goin through that floor, sure as youre born. Get out that door.' Mule looked at me sad-like and then just disappeared. And in its place was my first wife, in the clothes she was buried in. She come up to me and I put my arms around her, but I couldn't feel nothin' (another sniff from the second wife) and I says, "Babe, what you want?"

Then she started to git littler and littler and lower and finally went right away through the floor. It was her spirit thats what it was. ("Rats" says the second wife.)

"Another time she came to me by three knocks and made me git up and sleep on another bed where it was better sleepin'."

"I like to go back down in Kentucky on visits as the folks there wont take a thing for bed and vittles. Here they are so selfish wont even gave a drink of water away."

"Yes'm the flood got us. Me and my wife here, we whet away and stayed two months. Was 5 feet in this house, and if it ever gets in here agin, we're goin down in Kentucky and never comin' back no more."

The old man and his wife bowed me out the front door and asked me to come back again and we'ed talk some more about old times.

www.ingramcontent.com/pod-product-compliance
Lightning Source LLC
Chambersburg PA
CBHW060252100426
42742CB00011B/1727